Costume in Greek

COSTUME
IN
GREEK TRAGEDY

Rosie Wyles

Bristol Classical Press

First published in 2011 by
Bristol Classical Press
an imprint of
Bloomsbury Academic
Bloomsbury Publishing Plc
50 Bedford Square
London WC1B 3DP

CIP records for this book are available from the
British Library and the Library of Congress

ISBN 978-0-7156-3945-0

Typeset by Ray Davies
Printed and bound in Great Britain by
CPI Group Ltd, Croydon, Surrey

www.bloomsburyacademic.com

Contents

Acknowledgements

I welcome this opportunity to thank the many individuals and institutions who have helped me in the production of this book. If I go back to the beginning, then I must thank my Latin teacher, Louise Pavey, and drama teacher, Jan Trevithick, who first introduced me to Greek tragedy. I have also been encouraged along the way by Matthew Leigh. I am grateful to everyone at the Archive for Performance of Greek and Roman drama, Oxford, and especially to Oliver Taplin and Edith Hall to whom I owe much; Edith has been an inspiration to me. Chris Vervain has been generous in both sharing her knowledge of masks and inviting me to be involved in one of her projects (which offered some helpful insights into costume). My gratitude goes to all the institutions and individuals who granted permissions for the images reproduced in this book. I am also grateful to the Jowett Copyright Trustees whose kind grant enabled me to include so many images. I am lucky to have had support from family and friends (especially Lizzie, Susannah and Alex); Susannah Wyles and Peter Olive deserve special thanks for their proof-reading. I am indebted to Perry Holmes who has offered me countless Havana mules and words of encouragement. I am also grateful to Deborah Blake at Bristol Classical Press for her enthusiasm and wonderful efficiency. Finally, I would like to thank my parents, Anne and Peter Wyles, who are a constant source of love and support, and to whom this book is dedicated in gratitude for everything.

R.W.

List of Illustrations

Introduction

Costume was one of the most significant elements in fifth-century performances of Greek tragedy. In these open-air productions which had no artificial lighting effects, we can imagine that much of the visual impact came from the masks, costumes, and props used to represent the characters on stage. But the significance of costume goes beyond its contribution to the visual or aesthetic aspect of tragedy, since, in fact, it played an essential part in the creation of meaning in these productions. It is this that makes it so important for us to try to understand how costume works, because by understanding it, we may come to a closer appreciation of the Greek tragedies. The fifth-century playwrights themselves display an interest in the theory of what is now termed 'semiotics', the signs used in a performance, and within their plays explore the question of how costume operates. In the development of tragedy over the fifth century, the tragedians are busy establishing this type of theatre's style, content, conventions, and artistic territory, but they are, at the same time, experimenting with costume and determining how best to use it in tragedy. What emerges by the end of the fifth century is a sophisticated language of costume, capable of producing many different dramatic effects, layers of meaning, and comments on theatre. This language of costume, and the techniques for its exploitation developed by the fifth-century tragedians, form a part of the foundations for semiotics in our theatre today.

The importance of thinking about the staging of tragedy as part of the process of interpreting these ancient plays has long been accepted; Oliver Taplin's *Stagecraft of Aeschylus* (1977) was the first major work in the English language to highlight the importance of this. In the wake of this acceptance, the need for a book on costume in Greek tragedy has long been apparent (see Goetsch 1995). But even so, nothing comprehensive has yet been written. Although in recent years there has been a growing trend towards studying dress in the ancient world (e.g. Llewellyn-Jones 2002; Cleland et al. 2005; Sebasta and Bonfante 1994; Croom 2000; Edmonson and Keith 2008), there has not been the equivalent number of studies dedicated to theatre costume. Some of this work on dress nevertheless offers essential background and context, while the A-Z of Greek and Roman dress produced by Cleland et al. (2007) is also a valuable resource. Important too are the individual contributions in related areas, such as Barber (1992) and Vickers (1999) on weaving, and Reinhold (1970) on purple. Also extremely helpful is Linda Roccos' annotated bibliography on

1

ancient dress (which includes works on theatre costume), which makes the navigation of the scholarship in this area far easier (see Roccos 2006).

A glance at Roccos' bibliography shows that there is a reasonable amount written on tragic costume, but it is all in different places, some rather inaccessible, and the scholars are usually interested in focusing on one particular aspect of costume. The best general discussion of tragic costume is still Pickard-Cambridge (1968, 177-209), which also includes pictures of much of the visual evidence. But it is not within the scope of that work to discuss the semiotics of costume or to explore fully how it was used in performance. Bieber's (1961) discussion of costume now seems rather dated (especially in the emphasis she gives to ritual or religious considerations), but nevertheless includes a wide range of evidence and illustrations. A very brief, but useful, overview of costume is offered in Ley (1991, 17-22 with plates), and some insightful comments are made in the discussion by Green (2002) on costume in relation to performance style. Discussions of the visual evidence for tragic costume and assessments of the issues with this type of evidence can be found in Pickard-Cambridge (1968), Green (1991), and Taplin (2007).

As well as these general discussions of tragic costume, there has been work done on specific aspects of costume, its use in particular tragedies, and the costume-related Aristophanic scenes. Over 50 years ago now, Alföldi was engaged in trying to explain the development in the design of tragic costume (Alföldi 1955). The examination of costume in specific plays includes Thalmann (1980) on Aeschylus' *Persians*, Griffith (1988) on Aeschylus' *Oresteia*, and Marshall (2001a) on Euripides' *Hecuba*. As well as these articles, there are often isolated comments on costume in the commentaries on the individual tragedies. Two extremely insightful articles, on different aspects relating to costume, have contributed much to the area: Muecke (1982a) on disguise and Battezzatto (2000) on ethnicity. Analysis of pertinent Aristophanic scenes is offered by Macleod (1974), Muecke (1982b), Robson (2004), (2005), and Duncan (2006).

All the above discussions have some excellent points to make about tragic costume, but they are not intended to be comprehensive studies. In fact, the only study (in English) of tragic costume is Iris Brooke's *Costume in Greek Classical Drama* (1962), which gives a helpful guide to Greek dress but does not offer a full overview of the visual evidence for tragic costume or a close analysis of how the costume is exploited to create dramatic meaning in individual tragedies. This kind of analysis *is* given, however, by Taplin (1978, 77-100), though his case studies relate exclusively to props and this discussion occupies only one of the chapters in his study. A more detailed and comprehensive study of tragic costume, and one which engages in some semiotic analysis, is offered in the German dissertation by Dingel (1967), but this work remains inaccessible to many. My own dissertation on tragic costume, Wyles (2007), was rather specific in its discussion and is equally not readily accessible. The most recent, highly sophisticated, work to emerge on tragic props is rather specialised, but shows an encouraging growth of interest in this area (see Chaston 2010). Meanwhile comic costume *has* been the dedicated subject of a study (see Stone 1980); further semiotic analysis of its use in performance has been offered in Revermann (2006). The area of masks has been equally lucky in the modern works which have emerged (see especially Wiles 1991, 2007; Vervain and Wiles 2001; Lambert 2008). Scholarship in this area is showing the beginning of a trend which looks at the issues, significance, and implications of mask in modern productions of tragedy; this is also an emerging concern in discussions of tragic costume (see Llewellyn-Jones 2001; Wyles 2010b).

The aim of this book, therefore, is to fill in some of these gaps and to tie together these loose ends. It is intended to offer a comprehensive introduction to what fifth-century tragic costume looked like and how it was used in performance. The majority of the evidence for tragic costume, visual and textual (no fabric evidence remains), is gathered together in this book. The visual evidence is discussed in Chapter 1 and each piece is illustrated. The textual evidence falls into two categories: references made within the play texts themselves and comments made in later tradition. The references in the plays offer an excellent basis for the analysis of how costume was used in performance. Many of these references are quoted and discussed, especially in the discussion of how costume worked in Chapters 3 and 4, and they are all set out in the 'List of costume references' at the back of the book. The evidence offered by these references in the plays comes with two caveats. Some of the references, at least, seem likely to be metaphorical; so, for example, in Aeschylus' *Suppliants*, it seems probable that the Danaids' reference to tearing their veils (120-1 and 131-2) is metaphorical, rather than literal. So, each reference needs to be weighed and treated with caution in this respect. Also there are some costuming effects which are simply not commented on, but which must have had some visual impact in performance (even if they did not necessarily have dramatic significance); so, for example, we could guess that the costumes of Iris and Lyssa (Madness) in Euripides' *Heracles* must have been striking. The references in the texts, therefore, can only reveal something to us about the costumes which were made dramatically significant within the play. Even with these two caveats in mind, the references to costume in the play texts are the best evidence for the operation of costuming strategies in fifth-century tragedy. The other textual evidence, external to the plays, is generally late and unreliable, but the most important passages are, nevertheless, given in the Appendix.

As well as offering an overview of the visual evidence in Chapter 1, the practicalities of costume as a material object are considered in Chapter 2. For the rest of the book, costume is thought about in both material and symbolic terms. The ideas of semiotics, treating costume as a sign to be read in the performance, form the basis for the discussion of the language

3

of costume in Chapter 3 and the analysis of it in action in the plays in Chapter 4. It would have been impossible to discuss the use of costume in every tragedy, and therefore I offer a broad selection of representative examples (which show the principles of the language of costume in action). The discussion shifts focus in Chapter 5 to explore what the handling of costume in the plays shows us about fifth-century ideas about theatre. The final chapter examines the issues involved in translating costume, both in the Roman world and in modern productions, and the semiotic implications of certain responses to this challenge.

Throughout the discussion, I make the following distinction between costume and clothing: costume is what the actor wears, whereas clothing is worn by the character. Where I use a technical term for a piece of costume, it is italicised and a definition of it is given in the glossary at the back. References to scholarship are given throughout the text by the use of the author and date of publication shorthand, but the full reference for every work is given in the bibliography.

1

The Visual Evidence for Tragic Costume

This chapter offers an overview of the visual evidence for what costume looked like in ancient performances of tragedy. Representations of tragic actors appear on all kinds of artefacts in antiquity: vase paintings, reliefs, statuettes, wall paintings, mosaics, and even oil lamps. These representations offer invaluable evidence for what tragic costume looked like. Even if in many cases we are not being shown a play in action but rather a view of the actors before or after the performance, nevertheless we can learn much about the colour, patterning, and general design of costume from these representations. Without this evidence, it would be very difficult to know what tragic costume looked like at all, especially for fifth-century Athens, since the written sources about the development of tragic costume come from a later period and are not reliable (see Appendix). The tragedies themselves give clues to what particular costumes looked like and how they could be manipulated to create dramatic meaning (exploiting what I call the 'language of costume'), but in terms of the general picture for the appearance of tragic costume and its development over time, the visual evidence is our best guide. Of course, this evidence needs to be negotiated. It is not an exact record of what was on stage, but is a representation in a different artistic medium which is therefore set at a remove from reality. The image of what was seen in theatre is translated through the language of artistic convention into a representation which is set within the limits of a given medium and subjected to the individual viewpoint and whim of the artist. While keeping this limitation in mind, we will look at a range of visual evidence for tragic costume.

The evidence is ordered chronologically in order to give a sense of the developments in costume. This is not an exclusive survey and many other pieces of evidence exist, especially for the Roman period. What is offered here is some of the most important evidence, especially for fifth-century Athens, which as a representative selection can illustrate the major points about the appearance of tragic costume and should also, I hope, dispel some of the misconceptions about it (above all, notions of draped bed-sheets need to go). What will become obvious to the reader is that thinking in terms of one costume, 'the tragic costume', worn from tragedy's début in late sixth-century Athens and maintained throughout the century following, is misguided. In fact, costume, just like the tragedies themselves, seems to have been in an organic state of development over the fifth century. It is not even clear that by the end of the fifth century, tragic

Fig. 1. Tragic chorus of young warriors, 500-490 BC.

costume had settled on a fixed form, although the impact of the internationalisation of tragedy towards the end of the fifth century may well have acted as a catalyst to the process (on internationalisation of theatre see Csapo 2010, 83-116). By Roman times, however, the form had definitely stabilised and a tragic actor could be recognised easily through his costume which was by then very distinctive. It is perhaps this later clarity of form in the costume, and its close association with the genre's identity, that has encouraged people to think in terms of one tragic costume worn from the beginning and adjusted a little by the Romans. A look at the visual evidence shows that this scheme is too simplistic. Furthermore, as we will see in Chapter 6, even where the costume's form is kept the same, the responses to it and the way in which it is interpreted can shift dramatically between different cultures and different audiences.

Our earliest piece of evidence for tragic costume is an Attic red-figure column krater in the Mannerist style, dated to between 500 and 490 BC (Fig. 1). The vase seems to represent a moment from a tragic performance where the chorus of young warriors danced and sang in front of a tomb to raise the ghost of a dead hero (seen just on top of the tomb) (Green 1991, 34-5). The costumes of this chorus are a far cry from the draped white bedsheets which are often now associated with performances of tragedy. We cannot tell the colouring of the costumes from this red-figure representation, but there is no reason to assume that they were white. Furthermore the rather elaborate patterning of these costumes poses a challenge to the cliché of stark minimalism in tragic costumes (for this

6

period at least). The young warriors wear patterned *stephanai/diadems* (headbands), short *chitons* bordered with a stripe, and elaborately patterned corslets on top. The geometric maeander motif (the inverted 'L') which is used in the patterning of the *stephanai/diadems* and on the corslets echoes the patterning of the 'fillets' (ribbons/headbands) which have been left as offerings at the tomb. The palmettes (the motif which looks like an encircled peacock) which also decorate the corslets echo the use of the same motif on the vase's neck and are found used again in the fabric of a tragic costume over 90 years later as shown on the Pronomos vase (see Fig. 9). This patterning would have been woven into the costume since this was the primary way of decorating fabric in this period (see Chapter 2). We know of the existence of woven corslets from a surviving fragment of one found in the shaft graves of Mycenae, Homer's use of the epithet *linothorex* (linen-corsleted), and the story told by the fifth-century Greek historian Herodotus about a particularly spectacular corslet woven with gold (Herodotus, *Histories* 3.47). Furthermore, linen (as opposed to bronze) had become the dominant material in the period just before this vase was painted, *c.* 500 BC (see Everson 2004, 110-12 and 147), making it likely that this is the material used. The hypothesis is confirmed by the fringing at the bottom of the corslets which suggests that a woven fabric is being represented here (the fringes are formed from the left-over vertical threads at the end of the piece of weaving). Compare the fringing shown on some of the *himatia* on the Pronomos vase (Fig. 9), and on the end of the actor's *chiton* on the Gnathia fragment (Fig. 13).

While the pleats of the short *chitons* point to the kind of drapery that we might expect of Greek clothing, elements of this costume are more tailored. So, for example, the corslets are fitted with measured holes for the arms (rather than the wider gaps typically formed by draped garments). The tragic costume represented on this vase does not only challenge the modern stereotype of draped white bedsheets, but it also offers evidence against the assumption that elements which later became 'typical' of tragic costume were there from the beginning. Over the course of tragedy's performance history, long fitted sleeves, long robes, and then tragic boots (*cothurni*) would gradually come to be elements associated with tragic costume. But these features were evidently not yet essential to tragic costume, since this vase from the frst decade of the fifth century (and therefore not so distant from tragedy's inception in the last decades of the sixth century) does not show any of these features. The warriors are in short *chitons* without long sleeves and are not shown wearing any footwear at all. Even if we assume that on stage the chorus must have worn some footwear, it is not yet so closely associated with tragedy (as the boot would be later) for the artist to feel that he must depict it. From this it is clear that it runs against the evidence to assume a scheme where tragic costume's form was decided at the moment of the creation of this artform and remained the same thereafter.

The representation of the warriors with bare feet raises an important issue about what the artist is putting before our eyes in this type of representation. The line on the left ankle may hint at the painter's awareness that these chorusmen had footwear in the performance (see Green 1991, 35). This invites the question why the artist represented them barefoot, even though he knew (or we might suspect) that in the actual performance their costume included some kind of footwear. The explanation for this disparity is usually put down to the impact of performance – the audience watching a play sees what is on stage but also sees, in the mind's eye, what the playwright invites them to see. The performance creates another reality – a playworld where the action takes place. So when the artist comes to create his work, inspired by the performance, he may include elements both from the reality of the performance *and* from the imagined reality of the playworld. In the performance the chorusmen may have had footwear, but in the artist's imagination he remembers these figures (in their conjured form) as barefoot. This phenomenon has long been recognised by scholars and various terms are used to describe it: 'ambiguity between two realities' (Green 1991, 34f.); 'bifocal standpoint of the artist' (Beazley 1955, 313); and (to describe the related phenomenon of slippage between off-stage and on-stage viewpoints) 'melting' (Pickard-Cambridge 1968, 187). This issue affects several of the pieces of visual evidence for tragic costume and this certainly adds to the complexity of 'reading' the evidence and trying to establish what was actually worn on stage. At the same time, this very tendency to be drawn into the imagined playworld when representing actors in costume is revealing and can tell us something about the way in which tragic costume was viewed and how it worked (see Chapter 3).

Even though the artist may depict this chorus as the performance has invited him to imagine them (rather than how they really looked on stage), the faces of these chorusmen can be taken as a fair indication of masks since they show consistency with unambiguous visual evidence from the fifth century (see, for example, Figs 4 and 5). The most important observation to make is that the masks are naturalistic and are in real contrast to the masks used by Roman tragic actors. This naturalism to the masks in this period is also a challenge to modern preconceptions which expect the gaping mouth, wide eyes, and horrified expression often associated with tragedy. Instead we have a naturalistic-looking mask with regular features and neatly arranged hair, falling close to the head. These masks, like those shown in Figs 4 and 5, seem to be based on the 'helmet mask' model. This type of mask, as the name suggests, covers the whole head with the hair attached to the mask rather than being a separate wig. There needs to be some leeway for the actor to fit the mask over his head, which means that the mask is slightly bigger than a real-life head, but the exaggeration is marginal (especially compared with Roman practice). The representation on this vase reflects the impression of

8

naturalism that these masks gave. On the use of masks in performance see Wiles (2007).

Before leaving these warriors, it is worth noting the usefulness of this evidence as a representation of a chorus' costume. We have a series of chorusmen side by side and it can tell us something about the approach taken to the uniformity in the chorus. What is interesting about this image is that while the similarity between the costumes suggests at once that this group is a chorus, at the same time there is some variation. So while two of the chorusmen have patterned *stephanai/diadems*, the rest are undecorated. There are differences too between the corslets – the chorus-man on the end has one decorated exclusively with the geometric maeanders. Similarly, the chorusman in the middle has extra patterning (little crosses) on the skirt of his *chiton*. This chorus then has 'family resemblance' rather than exact uniformity. However 'accurate' the vase painter may have been about the details of the difference, the important thing is that he had an impression of variety in the chorus. If this representation is indicative of a general trend and reveals a tendency to give the chorus similar, though not exactly identical, costumes, then this has interesting implications for assumptions about the 'unity' of the chorus and its voice: the chorus may be saying or signing the same thing in unison, but if there is some visual distinction between them, then it changes the nature of that uniformity of voice and speech act.

Our next piece of evidence is some pottery fragments from an Attic red-figure hydria, found in Corinth and dated to *c.* 470-450 BC (Fig. 2). The fragments were first published by Beazley (1955) and are also discussed by Pickard-Cambridge (1968, 182-3). They show the performance of a tragedy (as the presence of the *aulos* player to the left of Fig. 2 indicates), in which oriental characters are gathered round a burning pyre on top of which is another oriental character. These fragments offer excellent evidence for how oriental costume was represented on the tragic stage in the second quarter of the fifth century. The costume of these characters consists of: the *kidaris* (floppy hat, see Fig. 2a), trousers, and a patterned top with a long-sleeved garment (differently patterned) under it. The character on top of the pyre also has a dark scarf with a light border hanging down from around his neck and perhaps carries two sceptres (though this is not sure) which would suggest that he was a king. Two of the other characters carry a sickle-shaped instrument or weapon as seen in two fragments (see Fig. 2, bottom centre and left).

The *kidaris* and trousers are already sure indications, or 'strong markers', that these costumes are used to represent oriental characters, but the patterning of the fabric is also distinctively oriental. The patterns which are woven into the fabric include: lozenges on the trousers and at the top of the sleeve of the figure in the top left fragment, a black circle with a brown dot on the tops, and another motif (which is difficult to make out) on the main part of the sleeve on the figure in the top left fragment. These

Fig. 2. Fragments showing tragic costume of oriental characters, *c.* 470-450 BC.

Fig. 2a. Close-up showing *kidaris* and patterning of fabric.

motifs all carry strong oriental associations, as does the zig-zag (not shown here), and so would suggest to the audience that these characters were oriental. This evidence is particularly valuable as a sure representation of tragic costume for oriental characters, since it may offer a litmus test for assessing the 'oriental' costumes in other representations (so, for example, the costume of one of the actors on the Pronomos vase, Fig. 9 below). It is also worth noting that although this is one of our earliest pieces of evidence to show tragic costume with long fitted sleeves, here the sleeves are used in the costume in order to give ethnic colouring and indicate that the characters are oriental. Later on it would be for a different reason that long fitted sleeves were used in tragic costume (see Chapter 4); these fragments should not therefore be seen as a starting point for the more widespread inclusion of sleeves in the tragic costume.

The next three vases, Figs 3, 4, and 5, illustrate the tragic costume used for maenads (the female worshippers of Dionysus). The first is an Attic red-figure pelike dated to *c.* 460 which shows a maenad brandishing the torn-off leg of an animal in her left hand and a sword in her right. The *aulos*-player facing her indicates that vase represents a theatrical performance. The vase is discussed by Beazley (1955, 312), Pickard-Cambridge (1968, 182), and Green (1997, 33-4). Pickard-Cambridge is sceptical about how much the vase can tell us about tragic costume, since the chorusman has 'melted completely away' (on this phenomenon of 'melting', see above). The 'melting' has admittedly had an impact on the way in which the costume is represented: it results in not only the problematic issue of bare feet again, but also even a bare breast! The actors of tragedy in fifth-century Athens were male and we have no evidence of padding being used for tragic costume in this period (though it was used for comic costume (see Fig. 11), and in the Roman period would be used for tragic costume too, see below); so the costume used on stage could not have corresponded exactly to the asymmetric breast-revealing draped *peplos* shown on the vase painting. But even if the image depicts the character as conjured in the imagination, rather than as literally represented on stage, this does not prevent it from being useful evidence for costume. What it reveals is that in this period, *c.* 460 BC, it was possible for tragic costume to leave the audience with an impression of free-flowing sleeveless drapery. Even if there were some other garment used in the performance along with this *peplos* (to keep the male performer covered up), nevertheless the costume's impact was such that afterwards it could be remembered without this extra garment and produce a representation where it 'melts away'. It is evident from this that the long fitted sleeves that would later be associated with tragic costume were not yet iconic enough to be a 'must' in a representation of a tragic performer; it was still possible to 'unthink' them (if they had been worn) and represent a tragic maenad in performance without any sleeves. It is also notable that tragic costume evidently did not yet have to be full length.

Fig. 3. Maenad in tragic performance, *c.* 460 BC.

Fig. 4. Maenad in Ionic-style sleeved drapery, *c.* 460-450 BC.

12

Fig. 5. Tragic chorusmen putting on costumes, *c.* 440-30 BC.

The second tragic maenad vase, an Attic red-figure bell krater from *c.* 460-450 BC (Fig. 4), shows that drapery was certainly a possibility for the tragic stage in this period. In this case, both the maenad (figure on the right, presumed to be a member of the chorus) and the actor who holds the mask of the character whom he will play, wear full-length voluminous draped *chitons* with wide flowing sleeves in the Ionic style (cf. Fig. 17 in Chapter 2). The maenad's *chiton* is held in place by a fawnskin which is a typical attribute for a follower of Dionysus, whereas the chiton of the male character is held in place by the dark-bordered *himation* which is draped round and pinned at the shoulder with everything secured at the waist by a belt/'girdle'. The maenad's mask is again naturalistic and has a *mitra* (headband/snood), again apparently normal for maenads (Euripides, *Bacchae* 833), covering the hair. The maenad wears soft boots with turned-up pointed toes. The same style of boot is worn by the maenad chorus members in the next vase (Fig. 5), and there it is clear that this type of boot was knee-high. Importantly these boots have flat soles, unlike later tragic boots. Although they fit the fifth-century definition of *kothornoi* – a term which was used to refer to soft boots which were loose enough to be pulled onto either foot and were associated with women, they are not the same as the platform-heeled tragic boots (*cothurni*) which were iconic in

13

the later period. In the fifth century it seems to have been the role being played, i.e. female maenads, rather than the type of drama, which dictated the inclusion of these boots in the costume. An excellent example of how different footwear could be used to define and contrast individual characters is offered in Euripides' *Orestes*, in which, it seems from the eunuch's speech (1369-72 and 1467-70), Helen wore golden sandals, the messenger wore Persian slippers, and Orestes wore Mycenaean boots (see Chapter 4).

The final vase showing the costume of tragic maenads (Fig. 3), is another Attic red-figure pelike, this time dating to *c.* 440-430 BC. Its image confirms that some 20 or 30 years after our first maenad vase (Fig. 3), the sleeves of the costume were still negligible in representations; i.e. sleeves are not yet so closely associated with the costumes of the tragic world that they must be included in illustrations of tragic actors (alternatively they were not part of the costume at all, but this invites similar conclusions). The vase shows two chorusmen getting dressed in their costumes: the one on the left is fully costumed and already in character, while the other on the right is pulling on his boot and is yet to put on his mask. The main costume again leaves an impression of drapery (as opposed to the fitted costumes). The chorusmen wear simple Doric-style *chitons*, folded round, pinned at the shoulder (see the chorusman on the right) and with the dark-bordered edges of the fabric meeting at the side (cf. Fig. 18 in Chapter 2). These *chitons* are hitched up and must be gathered up in a belt/'girdle', which gives the bulging fold in the skirt. The hitching up of the *chitons* allows for greater movement but also allows for the possibility of full-length costumes at some point in this play. The costume for these maenads also included a *himation* (wrap) which the chorusman on the left holds bundled up in his hand. Presumably this *himation* too could have been used to change the appearance of the costume during the play – being at some points wrapped round, at others integrated into the chorus' movement (as it is here) and at others still perhaps discarded.

This vase offers valuable evidence for tragic masks, since quite exceptionally there is a mask shown in profile, resting on the ground between the two chorusmen. From this, it is confirmed that the helmet-model was used for masks (see above). There is little exaggeration and the features are still naturalistic (as the images so far have already suggested). The vase also gives a clue to the practicalities of wearing the mask by showing the headband, to be worn under the mask, which therefore made up part of the performer's kit, though not of the character's outfit.

The variation shown between the costumes represented in this series of vases (Figs 3-5), underlines the major point that tragic costume did not yet have a fixed form during the fifth century. It is not only that there is not yet uniformity in the general design of tragic costume (compare, for example, the costumes in Figs 1 and 2 with those on these vases!) but even for the same character type the costume was not restricted to one form.

1. The Visual Evidence for Tragic Costume

While there are points of similarity between the maenads' costumes – such as the soft turned-up pointed boots and the general impression of drapery – there are also important differences. There are the optional extras: a sword (Fig. 3), the fawnskin (Fig. 4); the difference in hairstyle: long-flowing (Fig. 3), *sakkos* (Fig. 4), and headscarf (Fig. 5); and the difference in style of drapery: Ionic (Fig. 4) vs Doric (Fig. 5). During the central decades of the fifth century tragic costume was finding a form through experimentation and through different types of costuming being tried out on the tragic stage. It is not even that we can project a neat scheme where there was a general 'drapery phase' in tragic costume during this middle period, since while, evidently, drapery did appear on the tragic stage at this time, we also have evidence to suggest that other types of costumes were making their appearance alongside it. One example is offered here in Fig. 6. This Attic red-figure pelike is one of a series of five vases dating to the 440s which seem to have been inspired by, or produced in response to, the performance of Sophocles' *Andromeda* (see Green 1991, 42-4). The tragic heroine, Andromeda, is shown in an oriental costume with zig-zag patterned trousers and sleeves, a short belted *chiton* (decorated at the bottom) and the *kidaris* (floppy hat). While this evidence for tragic costume is not as strong as the vases showing actors and chorusmen off-stage (where the masks placed separately make it clear that we are looking at figures in theatrical costume), it can still suggest something about the impression made by the tragedy. As a response to the production, it shows that the tragic world did not necessarily have to be imagined as inhabited by draped figures. So that, rather than thinking of the maenads' costumes as generally indicative of tragic costume in this period, it is more helpful to think of drapery as one of the possibilities for tragic costume and one of the 'modes' in which the tragic world could be represented. It is even possible that drapery was considered particularly fitting for maenads whose free-flowing hair was used to express their liberation (see Euripides' *Bacchae* 695). At the same time, certain drapery might be used to create a sexual dynamic in the tragic worlds of other productions (see Marshall 2001a).

Another mode for representing tragedy is suggested by the Attic red-figure bell krater fragment, found in Olbia and dating to *c.* 430-420 BC (Fig. 7). The female chorus wears *stephanai/diadems* in their hair and fitted patterned costumes which are in contrast to the plain drapery of the maenads. Though they are not 'fitted' in the sense of being tailored close to the body, there is a defined neckline, the side seams must be sewn, and the finished *chiton* is drawn in at the waist by a patterned 'girdle'/belt. It is not clear from the available images of this fragment whether these costumes had long fitted sleeves reaching down to the wrist, though the patterning around the armhole certainly invites this assumption (on the analogy of the oriental figure in the top left fragment in Fig. 2). If long fitted sleeves are a part of this chorus' costume, then it is not clear (given

Fig. 6. Possible tragic costume for Andromeda in 440s.

the limited context) whether they were there to suggest oriental accenting or whether this is the first instance of sleeves being used in tragic costume independent of such a semiotic function. The *stephanai/diadem*s and the circle-patterning of the *chitons* perhaps make a stronger case for seeing the sleeves as part of a strategy for oriental accenting in the costume. It is also possible that this fragment offers the earliest piece of evidence

1. The Visual Evidence for Tragic Costume

Fig. 7. Tragic costume for female chorus, c. 430-420 BC.

for the use of full-length patterned and fitted tragic costumes, although this depends on the interpretation of the bordered skirt hem of the figure on the right; the hem seems to be hitched up to rest on the knee but may or may not have reached full length when the performer stood up straight.

The fragment also offers a clue about masking, since this female chorus have their faces painted white. The use of the convention of whitened masks for females, who spent most of their time indoors, is also shown on the Pronomos vase (Fig. 9) and the fragments now in Würzburg (Fig. 12). In the case of characters like the daughters of Danaus, who were from Egypt, the mask might be painted darker (certainly their male cousins are described as having dark skin (Aeschylus, *Suppliants* 719-20). In general, the contrast in the shading of female and male masks could offer the audience a ready index for assessing the gender of a character when they first entered; as tragic costume became more uniform, this shorthand, or semiotic coding, presumably became increasingly useful. It is also possible that the masks could give a hint of where a character was from (Aeschylus, *Suppliants* 278-83) or his/her status (Sophocles, *Electra* 664), simply through its features.

Whether the fragment from Olbia shows full-length costumes or not, we have sure evidence for floor-length tragic costumes from the end of the fifth century. The Piraeus relief dated to c. 400 BC (Fig. 8), shows performers in an off-stage setting holding their masks in their hands and in the presence of Dionysus, the god of theatre, who reclines on the couch in front of them. The three figures standing at the end of the couch have been identified as tragic chorusmen. The masks held by two of them are in proportion with their bodies and are, so far as it is possible to make out

Fig. 8. Costume of tragic chorus on Piraeus relief, *c.* 400 BC.

details, naturalistic with regular features. This is the first piece of evidence to show the tragic costume in the design which would become 'typical'. The robes are full-length and use a generous amount of fabric which, gathered in at the waist by a 'girdle'/belt, creates pleats in the skirts. The costumes have high necks and fitted wrist-length sleeves. Even though the marble of the relief is too worn to be able to give us any idea of the fabric's patterning (its colours or motifs), it is very useful in showing the emergence of features which would become common.

The Pronomos vase (Fig. 9) named after the *aulos*-player who sits in the middle of the bottom row of the figures on the side of the vase shown here, is one of the most informative, and challenging, pieces of evidence for costume to survive from antiquity. This large Attic red-figure volute krater was found in South Italy and dates to *c.* 400 BC. Actors and chorusmen are shown relaxing off-stage, with masks removed, in the presence of Dionysus who reclines with Ariadne on the central couch. The chorusmen have just played in the satyr drama (the last play in the performances of tragedy) and are wearing the characteristic costume of satyrs: furry trunks with a *phallus* attached at the front and a horse tail at the back (visible in the costume of the satyr who dances to the left of the seated *aulos*-player Pronomos). The satyr masks are characterised by their snub noses, pointed ears and beards. The vase also shows two actors who are still wearing their stage costumes, but who hold their masks in their hands. The costumes of these two figures, shown in detail in Figs 9a and 9b, offer good evidence for what would be worn for performances of tragedies, on the assumption that there was continuity between satyr drama and tragedy in this respect (see Pickard-Cambridge 1968, 180).

Fig. 9. Pronomos vase showing actors in tragic costume.

The masks of both characters are again naturalistic and well in proportion with the actors; they evidently do not yet leave the impression on the audience, or the artist, of being over-sized as they would later. We can also learn another practical detail from this image, since it shows the strings by which they were carried around. It has previously been assumed that the mask of the actor on the left (Fig. 9a), has a *tiara* on top of it. But this is a misreading of the image which has been perpetuated by the frequent reprinting of Reinach's image of the vase (it is used, for example, in Pickard-Cambridge 1968, fig. 49), in which the mask string was restored to look like a *tiara*. If we compare his mask to the white-painted female mask held up by the woman at the end of the couch, which *does* have a *tiara*, then the difference clearly shows that the line of the male mask in Fig. 9a must represent a string.

The question whether this actor holds a mask with a *tiara* or not, raises an important issue about identifying 'oriental' tragic costume in images. The process by which the character played by the actor on the left (Fig. 9a) became dubbed 'an oriental king', is telling. The female mask with its *tiara* suggests that the play was located in a 'barbaric' land or was based in Greece but had oriental characters in it. This assumed setting invites the

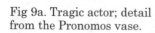

Fig 9a. Tragic actor; detail
from the Pronomos vase.

interpretation of the mask's string as the outline of a *tiara*, which would suggest that this actor played an oriental character, and the elaborate patterning of the costume's fabric seems in keeping with this. Yet, without the assumption of a *tiara* on the mask, there is no decisive element in the costume from which to determine the character's ethnicity. The costume is highly patterned, but there is nothing overtly 'oriental' about the motifs (in marked contrast to the fabric patterning on the fragments found in Corinth: Fig. 2). Instead of the typical oriental motifs (lozenges, zig-zags, and circles and dots), we find on this actor's costume: horses, the wave (*parakymatios*), winged *eros* figures, the *psi* motif (like an inverted cactus), and palmettes (like an encircled peacock). Many of these patterns are also used on the costume of the other actor on this vase, who plays the part of Heracles (Fig. 9b). If Heracles, the archetypal Greek hero, can wear clothing with this patterning, then there is nothing to suggest that it would be perceived as inherently oriental to have very elaborate fabric on stage; in real life a prized ritual artefact and focus point of Athenian civic identity was the elaborately patterned *peplos* made in honour of Athena each year as part of the Panathenaea festival (see Vickers 1999, 29). The whole question of whether a tragic costume is oriental or not is a complex one, but as a general rule if there are no 'strong' markers of orientalism, such as the *tiara*, trousers, or typically oriental motifs (dots, zig-zags and lozenges), then it is fairer to remain open to either possibility. In fact, what often determines the interpretation of a costume is how it is perceived and treated within the play itself (see Chapter 3), so without the context of the playworld (created by the words of the play) many images of costumes remain ambiguous.

If the costume of the actor on the left (Fig. 9a) is not particularly oriental, then what can it reveal about tragic costume at this point (c. 400 BC)? The costume, made up of a *chiton* and *himation*, is long-sleeved, long, and fitted in a design similar to what can be made out on the Piraeus relief (Fig. 8). This offers a real contrast to the looseness of the costumes that were used for the maenads (Figs 3-5 above). Similarly the elaborate patterning of the fabric presents a striking contrast with the plainness of the fabric used in their costumes. The costume here is closer to the impression of the costumes given by the fragment from Olbia (Fig. 7), which are also fitted and gathered in at the waist by 'girdles'/belts of a similar design to the one shown in this actor's costume. While the patterning of tragic costume would continue to vary (in terms of both design and intensity), this actor offers a very clear representation of a design of costume, i.e. the long-sleeved, fitted, ankle-length costume, which would become typical for tragic actors.

In a related point, it is important to recognise that while the *chiton* of the tragic actor's costume may have begun to find the form which would later become iconic, at this stage the design was not uniformly applied. So, for example, if we look at the other actor on the vase who wears the

Fig. 9b. Heracles; detail
from the Pronomos vase.

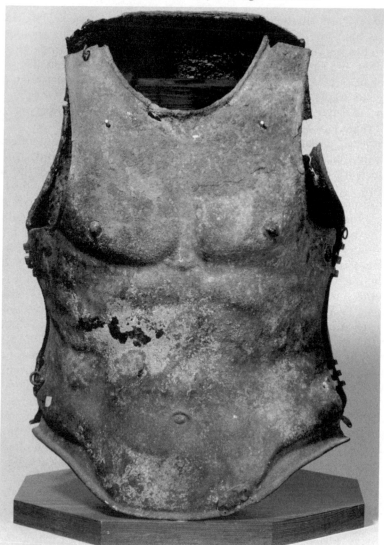

Fig. 10. Bronze muscle cuirass from the fourth century BC.

costume for Heracles there are similarities with the other costume but also important differences. The patterning of the fabric repeats some of the motifs which we have already seen on the other costume, and the *chiton* is long-sleeved and fitted, but it only reaches down to the knee (cf. the costume of the actor on the fourth-century Gnathia fragment, Fig. 13). The other differences in costume are determined by the specific character to whom it belongs. Heracles is a renowned warrior and therefore his costume includes a breastplate and patterned greaves to protect his shins (some interpret these as boots reaching up to the knee: see below). He also carries his bow (the top curve of which is just visible by the shoulder on the right), and quiver (the case for the arrows, which is slung across his shoulder and rests above his hip), his lion skin, and his club. These last pieces of costume were so strongly associated with Heracles that when Dionysus wants to disguise himself as this hero, in Aristophanes' comedy *Frogs*, he simply adds these bits of costume to what he is already wearing (with ridiculous consequences!).

Heracles' breastplate is worth further comment, since it offers an important clue to both costume design and the conceptualisation of the tragic world constructed on stage. The artist has depicted the actor wearing a bronze muscle cuirass as part of Heracles' costume. As the name suggests these breastplates were closely fitting and moulded to suggest the anatomy of the soldier beneath; this was done through *repoussé* work (i.e. by beating out the shape) (see Everson 2004, 140-5). We have a surviving example of this type of breastplate dating to the fourth century BC and found in South Italy; it is now in the British Museum (Fig. 10).

The inclusion of this piece of contemporary armour as part of a tragic costume has important implications for our understanding of costume design and tragedy. This breastplate challenges the idea of a fixed form of tragic costume and supports the idea that costume was in fact changing over the course of the fifth century. Evidently even by the end of the fifth century, it was still possible to incorporate newly emergent pieces of dress into tragic costume – it was not yet too rigid for this kind of spontaneous development in its wardrobe. There was also clearly not a problem over the 'anachronism' which the inclusion of this fifth-century piece of armour implied. The view of the 'past', constructed through the words, costuming, and scenery of the tragedy, was far more fluid and forgiving than the modern attitude towards period drama, which puts critical emphasis on the necessity for historical accuracy. The audience of Greek tragedy was arguably more sophisticated in this respect and when thinking about tragic costume, we need to remember that our concept of 'historical accuracy' is alien to it.

One final element of these actors' costumes, which is worth mentioning briefly, is the footwear. Discussions of the vase often refer to the *kothornoi* (boots) worn by the actors, but this is not a very accurate or helpful term to use in this particular case. Looking closely at Heracles' footwear (Fig. 9b), it is possible to interpret it as a pair of elaborately decorated greaves (which lace up the side as the eyelets marked in white suggest) and flat-soled shoes with a turned-up pointed toe (see Wyles 2010b, 237-9). As for the other actor on the left (Fig. 9a), the design of his footwear is not very clearly shown, though the boots are flat-soled and with pointed turned-up toes. We have already seen examples of *kothornoi* in the maenad costumes of the chorusmen (Figs 4 and 5). In those cases the term is appropriate because the type of boot shown in the images fits the definition

Fig. 11. Stereotypically tragic Aegisthus on the Choregoi vase.

of *kothornoi* (soft pointed flat-soled boots which could go on either foot and were associated with women). The term is not appropriate to the 'boots' shown on the Pronomos vase, since they do not fit the description (they are too close-fitting). The second problem is that the use of the term implies the assumption of the existence of a special boot particular to tragic performances (as the *cothurni* would be later) for this period, but this seems to be a case of falling into the trap of retrojecting the later phenomenon; there is no evidence for a special tragic boot at this point. It is, nevertheless, possible that boots were a common choice of footwear for male characters in performances of tragedy at this time. The evidence of the Choregoi vase, which shows an archetypal representation of tragic costume (see below with Fig. 11), and includes a pair of flat-soled lace-up boots, supports this idea. But even if this is right, it is still a question of selecting the type of boot according to the character (the difference between the maenad boots and Aegisthus' on the Choregoi vase is instructive) and boots are at this point neither platform-soled nor iconic (a symbol that could stand for the artform).

The red-figure Tarentine bell krater known as the Choregoi vase (Fig. 11) is a particularly valuable piece of evidence, since it shows us what was considered stereotypical for tragic costume at the beginning of the fourth century BC (the vase is dated to *c*. 390-380 BC). In fact, the vase represents the performance of a comedy, but it seems that in this play Aegisthus, who is on the left with one hand held up to his head and whose name is inscribed on the vase, acted as a representative for tragedy (see Taplin 1993, 55-63). For the dramatic scenario to be effective Aegisthus had to look very obviously and exaggeratedly 'tragic' so that the audience understood what he was intended to represent. Aegisthus' outfit here is, therefore, a stereotype of tragic costume. It shows some continuity with the emergent trends which have been identified so far; above all the elaborately decorated long-sleeved ankle-length *chiton* is strikingly similar in shape to those on the Pronomos vase (Fig. 9), and is similarly gathered in at the waist by a decorated belt (cf. also to the fragment from Olbia, Fig. 7). The boots (not *kothornoi*), like those of the actor(s) of the Pronomos vase, are still flat-soled, with turned-up pointed toes. But there are also variations such as the fringing at the end of the *chiton*, the type of motifs used in patterning the fabric, and the inclusion of further accessories in the costume: a cloak worn over the shoulders, crossbands, a hat (*pilos*), and a ring worn on his right hand. He also carries both a sword (its hilt is just visible on his left side) and two spears. Weapons, in general, seem to have been specially associated with tragedy, the content of which invited their frequent inclusion (see Revermann 2006, 40); they are represented as part of the costume on four of the vases discussed here (Figs 3, 9, 11, 13). If there was an association of weapon-props specifically with tragedy, then the weapons become a particularly strong marker in this context where their inclusion may automatically categorise the costume as tragic. There is also something potentially funny about their inclusion: the comic playwright exploits the tragic association of this prop to the maximum by giving Aegisthus both a sword and spears, in a deliberate and humorous overkill which may also have been amusing for what it suggested about this character (cowardly paranoia?).

There is possibly a hint of the oriental in this character's costume: with its fringing and the use of zig-zags on the sleeves. The similarity between his gesture and that of the figure in the fragment from Corinth (see above), could strengthen the case. But the orientalising is balanced out by the typically Greek dark-bordered cloak which the character also wears (cf. the bordered *chiton* of the maenad in Fig. 3 and the cloak worn by the otherwise naked figure next to the *aulos*-player on the Pronomos vase in Fig. 9). It is, therefore, as for the actor on the Pronomos vase (Fig. 9b), impossible to determine for sure whether this costume is intended to be oriental. In this case, however, we are helped by knowing who the character is (Aegisthus) and given the myth material associated with him, the balance tips against reading his costume as intended to suggest oriental origins (unless he were in a disguise). Instead any oriental flavour to the costume might suggest 'metaphorical orientalism', on which see Sourvinou-Inwood (1997) and Chapter 4. The idea is that the audience's prejudice against the stereotyped oriental and all the negative qualities associated with this stereotype could be evoked against a given Greek character in a play by giving a suggestion of orientalism in the costume.

1. The Visual Evidence for Tragic Costume

Another factor which has to be taken into account when reading this costume is the cultural context of the performance and the intended audience (both of the vase and the play). This vase was made in Tarentum in the south of Italy. This may, in part, explain the variations in this tragic costume. While the fringing, for example, may be included in order to communicate something about this particular character (such as hinting at oriental qualities), it is also possible that it was simply an element of the South Italian version of tragic costume. This idea finds further support from the costume of another tragic actor represented on a different fourth-century vase (now fragmentary) from South Italy (see Fig. 13); which includes fringing but carries no hint of orientalism. So it is possible that fringing was a standard feature to the costume in South Italian, and even Sicilian (it is possible the painter could have been influenced by them), performances of tragedy. If this is the case, then this is all the more striking since in Athens fringing retained an association with oriental dress (see Miller 1997, 159-60). The other feature of Aegisthus' costume on this vase, which is arguably 'typical' in the South Italian version of tragic costume, is the crossbands. This element of costume is shown worn by characters frequently enough on the theatre-inspired vases of fourth-century South Italy and Sicily, as to suggest that it was a distinctive part of tragic costume in this region and period; for numerous other examples including the Medea Cleveland krater, see Taplin (2007). This assumption of local elements in tragic costume is analogous to the likely use of local choruses in performances of tragedy in this area (see Taplin 2007, 7). What we are looking at on the Choregoi vase is not necessarily an Athenian view of the stereotypical tragic costume, but a South Italian one. There was potentially some distance between tragic costume as it appeared in Athenian performances and the impression of its 'typical form' on the other side of the Mediterranean in South Italy and Sicily.

The possibility that South Italy and Sicily had their own slight variations on tragic costume has some important implications. Again it warns against assuming one type of tragic costume over either a given time period or land area. Costume may have developed in one way in Athens but then have been adopted and adapted in different ways as tragedy spread across the Mediterranean world. There are some clear points of continuity with elements of the costumes represented on the fifth-century evidence, but there was evidently not yet a strictly fixed form of tragic costume (unlike later in antiquity when the special boots, *cothurni*, become a prerequisite to being a tragic actor). If we think about the idea of how tragic costume spread, then presumably this was through attending the festival and performances at Athens, through hearing about these, and through viewing vase paintings (like the Pronomos vase, Fig. 9, which was made in Athens but found in South Italy, or the fragment of a vase again made in Attica but found in Olbia, Fig. 7). Later, from the third century BC, the guilds of itinerant actors known as the Artists of Dionysus, who

Fig. 12. Elaborate tragic costume on Würzburg fragments.

performed tragedy across the Mediterranean world, must have done much to spread the idea of what tragic costume looked like and presumably encouraged a greater consistency in the universal view of it.

If we return to the fourth century, then while there is further evidence to support the impression given by the Pronomos and the Choregoi vases (Figs 9 and 11), that tragic costume could be highly elaborate in terms of the patterns woven into it, there is also evidence to counter the assumption that such elaborate costume was the only form of tragic costume for the entire century. The fragments of a volute krater now held in Würzburg and long said to be from Tarentum (though wrongly, according to Csapo in Taplin and Wyles 2010, 110), offers another representation showing elaborate tragic costume in this period (Fig. 12). This vase, now fragmentary, dates to around the same period as the Pronomos vase (Fig. 9), and like that vase shows figures off-stage, though still in costume and carrying their masks.

The actor shown sitting here wears a costume which shares features with both Aegisthus' on the Choregoi vase (Fig. 11), and also the actors on the Pronomos vase (Fig. 9). It is elaborately patterned, full-length, and gathered in at the waist by the same type of belt/'girdle' as we have already

Fig. 13. Short tragic costume on fourth-century Gnathia fragment.

seen. However, the Gnathia bell-krater fragment from Tarentum, South Italy (Fig. 13) dating from over 50 years later (*c.* 340 BC), suggests that there was variety in the form of tragic costume in this area. Again the representation is of an actor in an off-stage setting and holding his mask which helpfully confirms that we are looking at stage costume. His costume offers a striking contrast to those which we have just been looking at. He wears a short fringed *chiton* with long fitted sleeves and has a *himation* wrapped around his arm. He carries a sword in his left hand (turned inwards so that the hilt is visible) and he is wearing fur-topped lace-up boots. The most obvious difference is that his *chiton* is completely plain. There is no patterning woven into the fabric and the only decorative features are the white dots at the end of the sleeves and the fringing on the hem (discussed above). But before any ideas of bedsheets or minimalist marble-like elegance creep back in, this costume is not white but is coloured an earthy terracotta red (which contrasts with the colouring of the actor's flesh and the white hair of the mask). It is important that the *chiton* is not ankle-length but, like Heracles' on the Pronomos vase (Fig.

Fig. 14. Hellenistic tragic actor statuette with built-up mask.

9), comes down to the knee. Again this highlights the difference between tragic costume in this earlier period, where evidently there was more freedom of form, and the expectations of it in the Roman period. The Latin word frequently used to refer to tragic costume, *syrma* (which suggests the idea of something long and trailing) reveals the assumption of that society about the length of tragic costume. But our tragic actor on the Gnathia fragment reveals that in the mid-fourth century BC this was not yet considered a prerequisite. Similarly the mask is still naturalistic and his boots do not seem to have the later-fashionable platform-soles (so we can assume that their design has more to do with the character being played than the actor's identity as a *tragic* performer). The costume, unlike Heracles', is not so powerful as to force the artist to make the actor look like the character he is playing. In fact, there is a clear difference between the actor and his mask: the old man has a full white-haired beard, but our actor has stubble on his chin; shaving would be unusual in this period and so this detail suggests that the masks were more comfortable worn over a shaved chin (see Green 2002, 99).

The next piece of evidence, Fig. 14, is dated to *c.* 300 BC and reveals a major shift in the form of the tragic mask. The mask of this terracotta figurine of a tragic actor shows the exaggeration of features (gaping mouth) and the built-up hair-do (*onkos*) which become typical in the Roman period.

The difference between this mask and the old man's mask held by the actor on the Gnathia fragment (Fig. 13), is striking, and only 40 years, give or take, separate the two. This confirms the idea that tragic costume in the Roman period was the end result of an organic process of experimentation and development in costume during the first two centuries of tragedy's performance history. The costume of this actor shares features both with what has come before and with what would come after. The high, wide belt and the weight of the fabric (with the pleats it creates) recall the costumes of the performers on the Piraeus relief of 100 years earlier (see Fig. 8). The *chlamys* slung over the shoulder offers a variant on the longer cloak worn by Aegisthus on the Choregoi vase (Fig. 11). At the same time there are features that we have not yet seen and which would not become typical, such as the length of the *chiton* reaching beyond the knee but falling before the ankle. The boots here are much closer to the form that the *cothurni* would take – closer, for example, than the laced boots of our actor on the Gnathia fragment (Fig. 13) – although there is still some way to go since they are not yet platform-heeled.

The final form that tragic costume would take can be exemplified by another statuette, Fig. 15, this time in ivory and from a much later period (it is thought to date to the late second century AD). All the typical features of Roman tragic costume are shown here: the long-sleeved robe, the high wide belt, the elaborate fabric (here the blue robe is patterned with panel-stripes, coloured in blue and yellow, running down the front and

Fig. 15. Ivory statuette
showing Roman tragic
costume.

round the sleeves), the mask with exaggerated features and built-up hair (*onkos*) and platform-soled tragic boots (*cothurni*). All these features are confirmed as typical through their appearance in many other representations of tragic actors from this period (for examples see Bieber 227-53). The range of bright colours used for tragic costume is shown in tragic scenes in wall paintings and mosaics, many of which are preserved from Pompeii (see Bieber 1961, ch. 15, 227-53, and for colour plates of Pompeii see Coarelli 2002). There are also the textual references to the use of bright purple (Horace, *Epistles* 2.1.182-207) and gold (Lucian, *Wisdom of Nigrinus* 11, on which see Chapter 6). The mask of Roman tragic costume with its gaping mouth and exaggerated features may be a little closer to the generally held view of the appearance of tragic performances (since the mask with the downturned mouth is now an iconic symbol representing tragic theatre), but the variety of colour used in the costume is still a mental hurdle to the modern imagination of ancient tragic performances. For further discussion of Roman tragic costume and, in particular, its representation in the works of the second-century writer Lucian, see Kokolakis (1961), 33-42.

From this survey of the visual evidence for tragic costume within antiquity, a number of fundamental concepts become clear. First and foremost it becomes obvious that the generally held view of what tragic costume looked like is misguided – the evidence challenges the stereotype of simply-draped white sheeting. It is also obvious from the range of designs of costume shown in the representations that it is misleading to talk about 'the tragic costume' used in antiquity. There is a difference between Greek and Roman tragic costume, and even more importantly, for the study of Greek tragedy in its original performance context, there is variation in the representations from the fifth century (Figs 1-9). It is clearly not the case that tragic costume took up a fixed form at the emergence of theatre as an artform, nor that it was simply 'borrowed' from a different context. Instead the visual evidence points to a variety of costumes being put to use in different performances with perhaps only the hint of a more stable form towards the end of the century. Costume, like the artform itself, must have developed and emerged through an organic process of experimentation in the yearly productions. The visual evidence also suggests that the strict equation between character-type and costume, which Pollux's categorisation (see Appendix) implies, was not yet in operation and so must have emerged later. While the costume design in the fifth century seems to have been largely character-led (the choice being made on the basis of the character being represented), it was not yet a fixed system. From this point of view, the fifth century offered the playwrights a unique opportunity to experiment with costume and to exploit its potential to the full in their plays. We will look at their techniques for creating meaning through tragic costume in Chapters 3 and 4.

2

Practicalities

In the previous chapter, we looked at the available visual evidence for tragic costume and concluded that in fact, the design of the costume depends not only on the character being played, but also on the date of the production. There was not a fixed form of tragic costume in fifth-century Athens and the style of it could range from the drapery of the maenads' costumes (Figs 3-5), to the elaborately decorated fitted costume of the actors on the Pronomos vase (Figs 9a and 9b). This chapter takes some of that visual evidence and, synthesising it with the textual evidence, considers the practicalities of making and using tragic costume in fifth-century Athens. How was it made? What were the limitations on colours? What did different colours mean? What happened to costumes after the performance?

The major fabrics in ancient Greece were wool, linen, silk, leather, and felt. Specific items of costume might have been made of leather or felt. So, for example, there is reference to the leather jerkin (*diphthera*) of Argos as the normal wear for herdsmen in Sophocles' *Inachus* (fr. 281 *TGrF* with Lloyd-Jones 1996, 131). Also the hat (*pilos*) which Aegisthus wears on the Choregoi vase (Fig. 9) must be made of felt, and it is also possible that this fabric could have been used for parts of armour on the tragic stage, as it was in everyday life, on which see Forbes (1964), 92. A variety of animal skins could also be used in tragic costuming as references in the plays reveal: fox-skins for bacchants (Aeschylus, *Edonoi*, fr. 59 *TGrF*), fawn skins for bacchants (Euripides, *Bacchae*), lion skin for Heracles (Euripides, *Heracles* and Fig. 9b), and wolf skin ([Euripides], *Rhesus* 201-11 – not shown on-stage but seemingly could have been). The main body of the fifth-century costumes shown in the visual evidence in the previous chapter would have been made of wool or linen rather than silk – this can be deduced from the weight of the fabric (hinted at in the way it hangs), its patterning, and its opacity (there is no hint of silk's diaphanous nature). In this respect, the fabric of tragic costume forms a striking contrast with the scandalising silky costume used by pantomime dancers in Rome (see Wyles 2008). The plays themselves reveal that linen as well as wool could be used for costume: so, for example in Euripides' *Bacchae* 821 we are told that the dress which Pentheus changes into is made of *bussos* (a type of fine linen). For further references to linen costume in tragedy see the list at the back of this book.

The patterning which could be used to decorate the fabric of tragic costume, shown for example on the Pronomos vase (Fig. 9), would have been woven in. We learn from a passage in the fifth-century Greek historian Herodotus that weaving was the normal way of patterning fabric in ancient Greece. In a passage where he is talking about the people living in the Caucasus mountain range, he says (Herodotus, *Histories* 1.203, tr. De Sélincourt 1996):

> It is also said that there are trees here of which the leaves when crushed and mixed with water produce a dye with which the natives paint figures on their clothes, and the dye is so permanent that the designs never wash out but last as long as the material does, as if they had been woven into it when it was first made.

It is clear from this that the norm in Greece was to weave patterns into the fabric, since this method of painting on the patterns directly with a permanent dye is reported as being something extraordinary (and specific to the region). The normality of patterning fabric with elaborate designs through weaving is suggested by the scene in the *Iliad* where Helen is found in the midst of weaving all the woes of the war into a cloth (Homer, *Iliad* 3.121-8, tr. Lattimore 1961):

> Now to Helen of the white arms came a messenger, Iris,
> in the likeness of her sister-in-law, the wife of Antenor's
> son, whom strong Helikaon wed, the son of Antenor,
> Laodike, loveliest looking of all the daughters of Priam.
> She came on Helen in the chamber; she was weaving a great web,
> a red folding robe, and working into it the numerous struggles
> of Trojans, breakers of horses, and bronze-armoured Achaians,
> struggles that they endured for her sake at the hands of the war god.

Penelope is another epic heroine associated with weaving elaborate patterns (only to undo them again) (see Homer, *Odyssey* 2.94-110 and Fig. 16). These examples point to a world where the weaving-in of patterns was the established norm in the cultural imagination. So the patterning on the tragic costumes would be woven in rather than either dyed directly onto the cloth or added by embroidery. Threads would be dyed in different colours beforehand and then woven in as the fabric was produced, in order to create the patterns. Weaving in ancient Greece was done on the warp-weighted loom, illustrated in Fig. 16.

The warp (vertical) threads are kept taut by the use of a weight suspended at the bottom. The limited tension produced in this design of loom imposes restrictions on the kind of patterns which can be produced on it. Ideally motifs had to be based on a diagonal, like the maeander wave, and repetition in the patterning is also preferable (see Barber 1992, 111-12). The patterning which we have seen depicted on the costumes illustrated in the last chapter uses motifs which show both of these qualities.

Fig. 16. Penelope beside a warp-weighted loom on the fifth-century Chiusi vase.

The range of potential colours for tragic costume was limited by what could be produced from natural dyes. In this respect, it is necessary for us to rethink our rainbow spectrum and the assumption of a chemically-manufactured consistency to each colour. While many of the colours in the rainbow could be produced using natural dyes, there was not the same consistency in the resultant colour: so, for example, the 'purple' produced from the *murex* mollusc could be any shade within the general range of red, purple, and black (see Forbes 1964, 114, and Pliny, *Natural History* 9.60). Colour terms in ancient Greek therefore correspond to a much broader range of shades than our precisely-applied ones, e.g. mauve, violet, and indigo all refer to specific shades of purple. That is not to say that each colour and shade could not have a nuanced symbolic meaning, but simply that a greater number of shades could correspond to one colour term (based on the dye used). This fluidity of each colour-term's range must have been exacerbated by the fact that *murex*-purple was the only major dye to be colour-fast in antiquity (see Reinhold 1970). This explains why Herodotus is so concerned to emphasise the permanence of the tree-leaf dye (which was an exceptional quality) and it also suggests that

36

the natural process of colour fading in fabric contributed to the fluidity of notions of colour. In a world of fabric colours created through natural dyes, there could simply not be the same standardisation of each colour.

So if we rethink the rainbow, then rather than having seven strictly delineated shades, we need to think in terms of fewer bands (based on dyes) each covering a wider range of colours. This gives us: white, black/brown/grey/dark blue, red/purple/violet, red/orange/yellow (*saffron*), lighter blue/green/grey, frog green. To find out more about the dyes used in antiquity to make these colours and for the dyeing process, see Forbes (1964, 99-150). Our task of rethinking extends even further, since though we may have identified some of the equivalent colours to ours in antiquity, they did not necessarily 'mean' the same thing in the ancient context or carry the same associations. So, for example, while in our society pink is considered to be a particularly 'girly' or effeminate colour, in ancient Greece the equivalent colour was saffron yellow. Saffron (*krokos*) was strongly associated with females through ritual, and the saffron-dyed shift dress was a distinctively female garment (and therefore arguably the equivalent of our little black dress!); see, for example, Aristophanes, *Lysistrata* 219-22. Aristophanes exploits the feminine association of the saffron dress to humorous effect when he presents various male characters wearing one: Inlaw in the *Women at the Thesmophoria* (see especially lines 940-5); the god Dionysus wears it in combination with Heracles' weapons (giving a comic visual disjunction between the very masculine and very feminine elements of the outfit) in *Frogs* 45-8; and Blepyrus, who can find only his wife's to wear, in *Assembly Women* 331-2. There is some colour symbolism which remains the same between the tragic stage and our society, such as the use of black for mourning, used for example by: Electra and the chorus in Aeschylus, *Libation Bearers* 10-12; Helen in Euripides, *Helen* 1088 and 1186-7; the chorus in Euripides, *Suppliants* 97; and Tyndareus in Euripides, *Orestes* 457-8. But some very strong symbols from modern society, such as the white wedding dress, do not apply. In fact, the equivalent to a 'wedding dress' would be 'finery' (*kosmos*) which was general (and could be used on other special occasions) and was likely to be made of a colourful and elaborate fabric, in contrast to the typical use of plain white in our society (see further Chapter 4).

High status and wealth could be shown on stage through the use of expensive fabric; this is made explicit by the character Hermione in Euripides' *Andromache* 147-8 who refers to her fine/elaborately patterned (*poikilos*) clothing in her attempt to draw attention to her status. Cloth could be expensive either through the dyes used or for the elaborate work in its patterning; typical status symbols were sea-purple cloth (made using the juice of *murex* molluscs), such as the one famously trampled on by Agamemnon (Aeschylus, *Agamemnon* 958f.), or cloth with gold woven into it. It was even possible to produce fabric patterned with interwoven golden letters (see Vickers 1999, 20), though there is no evidence to prove that

Fig. 17. Drawing of Ionic *chiton* by Tom Tierney.

this was used in tragic costuming; the possibility, nevertheless, is intriguing. The motifs of the patterning, whether letters or not, not only had the potential to suggest wealth but might also convey more specific information about the character. The ability of such patterned textiles to communicate something to the viewer has attention drawn to it in Sophocles' tragedy *Tereus*, now lost, where Philomela, whose tongue has been pulled out, can only relate what had happened to her by weaving a patterned cloth (*poikilon pharos*, *TGrF* fr. 586). So, just as the design that Helen is weaving in the *Iliad* 3.121-8 is revealing, the motifs used in the patterning of a character's costume could presumably also hint towards his/her qualities or fate (I am grateful to Peter Meineck for this suggestion).

The fabric, once woven and patterned, then had to be put together to

Fig. 18. Drawing of Doric *peplos* by Tom Tierney.

make the costume. As we discovered in the last chapter, there was more than one design for tragic costume during the fifth century. Mostly we can assume that they were all designed in a way which would facilitate a quick costume change; costumes gathered in at the waist by a 'girdle'/belt, as many we have looked at are, were evidently loose enough to be put on easily over the head of the actor (before the mask). The 'girdle'/belt was also useful for allowing the length of the costume to be adjusted, since the costume could be hitched up into it (see Fig. 5). The draped costumes which are shown used for maenads in our visual evidence (Figs 3-5) are based on a rectangular piece of cloth being hung round the body and pinned. The two major ways of doing this in ancient Greece, were in Ionic or Doric fashion, as shown in Figs 17 and 18.

The visual evidence shows both styles of drapery being used for tragic costume: Fig. 5 shows Doric style draping and Fig. 4 shows Ionic. The Doric style is naturally more revealing (with one side left open and offering glimpses of the thighs) and yet the play texts support the visual evidence suggesting that it was used in performances. The give-away clue to the Doric *peplos* being used for some tragic costumes is the reference to dress pins (essential to secure this style of drapery) within some plays and use of those pins in the action, so that there can be no doubt that they were actually a physically-represented part of the costume: Oedipus will use Jocasta's dress pins to strike his eyes (Sophocles, *Oedipus Tyrannus* 1268-69) and Hecuba's attendants will use theirs (in combination with swords) to blind Polymestor and kill his children (Euripides, *Hecuba* 1169-71) (see Jenkins 1983 and Marshall 2001a). If the pinned, side-revealing Doric *peplos* was used in the costuming of Hecuba's attendants, Jocasta and others (as the vases and other play texts suggest), then it is possible that the actor would have worn a long-sleeved under-*chiton* (though we cannot know this for sure).

The fitted long-sleeved costumes which we have seen would have required more stitching than the drapery. The seams can be seen quite clearly running along the shoulders of the costume worn by the stubbly actor on the Gnathia fragment (Fig. 13), and there would also have been seams along the sides and sleeves. We do not have evidence for the type of stitching in use in this period, although button-hole stitch had been known since the Bronze Age (see Barber 1991), and so it seems likely that a simple running stitch could have been used to sew up the costumes. References in Aristophanic comedy suggest that sewing, as much as weaving, was recognised as an important part of the process in the creation of stage costumes. When, in Aristophanes' *Assembly Women*, the women want to disguise themselves as men, something which they have done in preparation is to sew together beards (lines 24-5). Since the use of disguise in a play can be read as a comment on the theatrical process of putting on costume (see Chapters 4 and 5), the reference to sewing their disguises in preparation can on one level be taken as a reference to the sewing of theatre costumes. Furthermore, elsewhere in Aristophanic comedy sewing is used as a metaphor for the poetic art of writing a play; this is brought out through the suggestion that Euripides creates plays by stitching together rags (see Macleod 1974 on Aristophanes, *Acharnians* 414-17 and *Frogs* 842). Again, this points to the consciousness of the important part played by sewing in the process of making theatre costumes and, by extension, creating theatre, since without costumes there could be no play (at least not in ancient Greece).

It is also in Aristophanic comedy that we find a reference to the people who made the masks used in productions; in Aristophanes' *Knights* 232, the *skeuopoioi* (mask-makers) are mentioned. The visual evidence in Chapter 1 suggests that the masks used in fifth-century tragic productions had naturalistic features, covered the whole head of the actor (using the 'helmet mask' design) and could be held in the hand using a string or strap. Masks were most likely to have been built up from linen rags, which were moulded and stiffened with glue, and then painted. Certainly from the perspective of a modern mask-maker it seems more likely that linen was used rather than cork or tree bark, as has sometimes been suggested (see Lambert 2008, 78-9). The reference to the women 'sewing together beards' for their male disguises in Aristophanes' *Assembly Women* 24-5, perhaps offers another clue to part of the process of mask-making since the hair, as we have seen in the visual evidence (see especially Fig. 9), was a fully integrated part of the mask. Unfortunately Aristophanes does not provide evidence for the material used to represent hair on the fifth-century theatrical masks and there is no clue in other ancient sources. Possible materials used for the hair of the masks include animal hair, wool, or even rope. Whatever material was used, it was evidently possible to produce quite a beautiful and realistic result, judging from the representation of perfectly coiffured hair on the Basel krater (Fig. 1). Pollux, who lived in the second century AD and records stage antiquities in Book 4 of his *Onomasticon*, offers a section explaining the categories of masks used in tragedy (see Appendix), but his comments do not readily apply to the fifth century BC when masks, like costumes, do not seem to have been so strictly regulated or categorised. The visual evidence shows a range of masks, but there is certainly not enough data to be able to argue for a specific system (though there are conventions). The plays themselves give clues to the different possible features of the mask: shorn hair for mourning and dirty hair (see the list at the back of this book for references), blinded eyes and, perhaps, blood (Oedipus in Sophocles, *Oedipus Tyrannus* 1298f. and Polymestor in Euripides, *Hecuba* 1056f.), and even horns ([Aeschylus], *Prometheus Bound* 674); but all of these features are dictated by the demands of the play rather than the stock character type to which Pollux refers. For a full discussion of Pollux on masks and different mask types in fifth-century tragedy, see Pickard-Cambridge (1968, 189-96).

The Greek term used in *Knights* for mask-maker, *skeuopoios*, could also technically be used to refer to prop-makers, since the Greek word *skeue* (which makes up the first part of this compound word and is above translated as mask) is a general term for equipment and could, in fact, be used to refer to the mask or the costume or the props, or all three together. But would the same term be used to refer to the weaver, who produced the often elaborate cloth for the tragic costumes? Since mask and prop making were very different crafts from weaving it seems unlikely that the term could be used to refer to the weaver too or unlikely that the same personnel were involved in both the mask making and fabric weaving (my thanks go to Elizabeth Barber for this point). Given the cost and numbers involved, even for the costuming in a single tetralogy such as the *Oresteia*, the manufacture of the fabrics would have been a serious commission demanding a separate team of professionals. It seems probable, on the analogy of the Panathenaea (festival in honour of Athena), that this commission would have been entrusted to a workshop of male weavers, who specialised in weaving *poikile* fabric (rather than being solely producers of theatrical costume); for Athena's *peplos* see [Aristotle], *Athenaion Politeia* 49.3 with Vickers 1999, 31-3 and Barber 1992, 113. In fact, it may be that the makers of elaborate cloth, the *poikiltai* (whom the politician Pericles is said to have introduced into the city (see Plutarch, *Pericles* 12.8 with Vickers 1999, 33), became involved in making the tragic costumes. The visual evidence certainly points to a phase of elaborate fabric in costuming in the last decades of the fifth century (see Chapter 1). Furthermore, within the tragedies themselves the cloth of the costume could be referred to as *poikilos* (so, for example, Hermione in Euripides, *Andromache* 147-8) and the much later (and admittedly problematic) textual evidence of Pollux suggests that, certainly at some point in antiquity, the main *chiton* of tragic costume was known simply by the term *poikilon* (elaborate/embroidered) (see Appendix). So this makes quite a strong case for assuming that, at least in the last decades of the fifth century, the men responsible for making the fabric for tragic costumes were known as *poikiltai* (workers of elaborate fabric). It also seems likely that the major undertaking of producing the fabric was a separate enterprise from the mask making. Even the production of the fabric could be subdivided between weavers and craftsmen for the other fabrics (such as leather and felt: see above).

If this is so and there were separate teams of craftsmen working on the masks, props, and fabric for the costumes, then this invites the question of who had control over the design of the costumes and harmonising the work between the mask-makers, prop-makers, weavers, and other fabric workers. We cannot know for sure, although it is tempting to suggest that the playwrights themselves took responsibility for this. Later traditions attribute an active role to the playwrights, not only in participating in productions (see *Life of Sophocles* 4 and Athenaeus 20e in Csapo and Slater 1994, p. 225) but also in the development of costume: in the *Suda* lexicon Aeschylus is said to have been the first to introduce sleeves, trailing robes and painted masks, and according to the *Life of Sophocles* 6, Sophocles brought in a particular type of white boot (*crepida*) (see Appendix and Pickard-Cambridge 1968, 205). The written sources for both of these claims are late and unreliable, but whether or not the playwrights were actually responsible for the specific innovations attributed to them, evidently it seemed plausible in this later period to imagine they had control over these matters. The idea of the tragedians' potential to offer stylistic input is also hinted at in the tradition that Euripides had been an artist before becoming a playwright (see *Life of Euripides* 17-18). These traditions perhaps reveal more about the period in which they were written than the fifth century BC, but even so there are already hints in the original context that the playwrights could be thought of as somehow in control of the costumes. This idea is implied in the scene in Aristophanes' *Acharnians* 393-489, where the comic hero, Dicaeopolis, borrows a tragic costume from Euripides whose house is full of them; on this scene see further Chapter 4. Inspiration for designs must have drawn on literary and artistic traditions (which informed audience expectation and provided some of the rules by which they decoded the visual information). But the design of a tragic costume could also draw on contemporary dress too, as we have seen already in the case of Heracles' breastplate (see Chapter 1, and on the implications of this see Chapter 4).

In terms of the practicalities of costume in the performance itself, the process of performers dressing up in their tragic costume is represented on the fifth-century Attic red-figure vase, now in Boston, showing two chorusmen dressing for their parts (Fig. 5). The most obvious order for the actor/chorusman to dress was: pulling on the *chiton* first over the head, gathering it in with the 'girdle'/belt, putting on footwear, adding any extra elements – such as the lion skin for Heracles (Fig. 9) or fawnskin for a maenad (Fig. 4) – and finally pulling the mask over the head (while a band possibly held the hair in place: see Fig. 5). We are also given clues about the process of dressing up in stage costume from the parodies of it which appear in two of Aristophanes' extant comedies: *Acharnians* 393-489 and *Women at the Thesmophoria* 212-79. The first of these is more explicitly engaged in commenting on dressing in costume since the comic hero borrows an actual tragic costume and puts it on, while the second example shows a man dressing up in disguise as a woman (though the close echoes of the scene from the *Acharnians* invite the audience to think of this disguise process in relation to theatre costume); on these scenes see Chapters 4 and 5. These parodies of the process of dressing in costume reveal how central Aristophanes considered costume to the creation of theatre, since through these scenes he examines the question of what theatre is and how it works. The treatment of costume in these scenes is also in keeping with his tendency to reveal the 'behind the scenes' of theatre to the audience in a very self-conscious way. So, for example, in Aristophanes' *Peace* 174, the comic hero Trygaeus comments directly on the crane-operator's lack of care. This, of course, could not happen in tragedy, and similarly all dressing up of performers had to take place off-stage for a tragic production. This is in stark contrast with pantomime performances later in antiquity, where tragic material was conveyed in dance by a solo performer who played all parts; in the case of pantomime, the transformation of the performer from one character into another and the minimal change in costume (switch of mask and perhaps also prop) was done in view of the audience and was part of the spectacle (see Wyles 2008). In tragedy, there could not be a hint of the actor or performer beneath the costume but the character had to remain ever-present while the actor was on stage (see Chapter 3). It is therefore only in off-stage settings (either before or after the action) that the vase painter is able to represent the performers with their masks removed (see Figs 5, 8, 9, 12 and 13).

The design of the theatre of Dionysus at Athens meant that the audience could see far more of the wings and beyond the stage than in a modern theatre, and it therefore seems most likely that the stage building would have been used for the purposes of getting dressed up in costume. This simple building at the back of the stage which was often used to represent a palace, was a part of the theatre from at least 458 BC (*Agamemnon*, the first play of Aeschylus' *Oresteia* trilogy, opens with a watchman delivering lines from the roof, which suggests the presence of a stage building at least by the date of this production). Since tragedies were performed using a maximum of three actors (and even fewer at an earlier date according to tradition), costume changes mid-performance were necessary to allow the same actor to play more than one part. These would presumably also take place in the stage building and could be made quite speedy by the use of costumes which simply went over the head, and were then gathered and secured at the waist by the 'girdle'/belt.

The Pronomos vase (Fig. 9) shows actors relaxing in the company of Dionysus and still wearing their costumes after the end of a performance, but what happened to the costumes after that? It is possible that the costumes, like the masks (see Green 1982), were dedicated to Dionysus; the dedication of clothing from outside the theatrical world is well-attested at the sanctuary of Artemis (see further Linders 1972 and Cleland 2005). If they were elaborate enough, and therefore capable of showing off Athenian *techne* (technical ability/craft), then perhaps they were put on display, as the Panathenaic *peplos* for Athena apparently was (see Vickers 1999, 32-3). There is also the possibility that costumes were kept and even reused. The scene in Aristophanes' *Acharnians* 393-489, where the comic hero, Dicaeopolis, goes to borrow a tragic costume from Euripides, and the reworking of this idea in Aristophanes' *Women at the Thesmophoria* 95-294, suggests that it was at least possible for fifth-century Athenians to imagine that these stage costumes continued to have an existence after performance and were stored by the poet (even if there is also clearly a metaphorical level to the idea whereby the costumes represent plays and a poet's repertoire). This idea gains further support from the scholiast's comment on Aristophanes' *Wasps* 1313 which tells us that the fifth-century tragic poet Sthenelos had sold his *skeue* (costume/kit), implying that playwrights were understood to keep a store of costumes. Later, in the third century BC, there is firm evidence from inscriptions to suggest that in parts of the Greek world individuals with collections of costumes were acting as costume-hirers: see LSJ s.v. *himatiomisthes* (costume-hirer). There is, however, no evidence for this in fifth-century Athens and it would seem contrary to the spirit of the Dionysia with its agenda of deliberate conspicuous expenditure (see Wilson 2000, 94). Though 'hire' seems out of the question, it does seem a possibility that some items may have been provided, rather than specially made, by the citizen-actors (or elite individuals wanting to win repute) and then taken back by them afterwards. This, for example, might explain the muscle cuirass used as part of Heracles' costume as represented on the Pronomos vase (Figs 9 and 10). As a contemporary piece of equipment and an expensive one since it was tailored for each individual (the shape was beaten out, using *repoussé* technique, to be a perfect fit), it is possible that it may have been the actor's own and simply 'borrowed' for the performance. Certainly later in antiquity professional actors owned and provided their own costume (which presumably had the potential to limit their repertoire), as is suggested by the epigram written in the first century AD by the poet Lucillius, about an actor selling his props to make some quick cash (*Anthologia Palatina* 11.189).

The importance of the practicalities of ancient tragic costume extends beyond the need to establish what kind of fabric was used or the types of designs that appeared on stage. Thinking behind the processes of fabrication reveals the necessity to rethink some of our basic assumptions about costume. So, for example, reflecting on the colours used and the natural dyes which were available to produce them, shows that the costumes were operating within a different system of colour. If we are to appreciate the costumes in the plays fully, then we need to rethink the colour spectrum and the cultural significance of the colours which form it. Even if there is only limited evidence about the fabrication of costume, hypothesising about the personnel involved suggests what a major undertaking this was and invites a reassessment of our view of tragedy as an enterprise: a greater part of the society contributed to its production than simply the playwright, *choregos* (chorus funder), actors and chorusmen. Similarly thinking around the issue of where the costume went after the production perhaps invites a shift in our view of the tragedian who in the cultural imagination was also keeper of tragic costumes. Moreover, the process of fabricating costume can have implications for the dramatic meaning produced by it within performances of the plays (see Chapter 4). An awareness of the practicalities of costume, therefore, has the potential to enhance our understanding of the plays, the cultural status of the production, and conceptions of the playwright.

Semiotics and the Language of Tragic Costume

So far we have been thinking about costume in fifth-century tragedy in a very material way. But in this chapter we will begin to think about how tragic costume operated on the symbolic level in ancient performances. Costume is not merely a physical presence in the production, but a bundle of visual data to be read and interpreted by the audience. In other words, costume is intended to communicate something and has its own 'language' (or code) through which to do this. These fundamental principles, for approaching costume and other aspects in the performance, were established in the 1930s and 1940s by the group of scholars known as the Prague school, who developed the theory of theatre semiotics. The basis of 'semiotic' analysis is to acknowledge that everything in a performance is a sign which is placed there deliberately (by the playwright or director) in order to communicate something to the audience. Following this premise, every piece of costume in an ancient performance was intended to signify something, either about the play setting in general or about a character in particular. The expectation that a person's clothing may carry clues about them is familiar from everyday life, where, consciously or not, we 'read' the clothing people wear and make assumptions about status, occupation, wealth etc., on the basis of it. But the major difference in the application of this in the theatrical frame is that there is a much greater self-consciousness about the use of a code, both for the playwright who is encoding (embedding symbolism into) the costume and for the audience who is decoding it. Both parties are conscious that a language of costume is being employed in a very deliberate and artificial way, while in everyday life the code may be more arbitrary, incidental, or even disparate. Theatre intensifies this experience of encoding and decoding by the heightened pressure on both processes (the success of the performance depends on both) and the concentration of signs (significant clothing) all in the same space; in this sense, the theatrical performance bears some similarity to a military parade, since here too every last detail of the clothing is predetermined and symbolic. If the onlooker is to appreciate such a parade fully, then he or she needs to be versed in the visual language or symbolic code being employed in order to understand, for example, what a certain medal signifies or the status designated by an epaulette. Similarly in ancient theatre, it was necessary for the spectator to be familiar with the language of costume in order to appreciate the meaning of the costume and, through that, of the drama. The decoding depended on a combination between

3. Semiotics and the Language of Tragic Costume

knowledge of clothing-symbolism from everyday life and, sometimes, more specialised experience of the use of costume in past tragic performances.

There is clearly a strong relationship between the process of reading clothing in everyday life and reading costume in theatre. The sensitivity of Athenian society towards the symbolism of clothing in everyday life may, in part, explain why theatre grew to be such a success in that city; since the audience could be responsive to costume as a theatrical sign and this allowed the playwrights to build up a sophisticated language of costume for tragedy. The perception of clothing as something of symbolic importance in Athenian society is already evident in the early sixth century BC, when Solon introduced sumptuary laws limiting the number of garments women could wear when travelling and the number of *himatia* with which a person could be buried (see Plutarch, *Solon* 21.4). This was part of an attempt to curb excessive displays of wealth (which could aggravate social tensions) and reveals the power that clothing held as a symbolic medium within the society in this early period. Its semiotic power continued well into the fifth century when we are told of the negative reaction that a member of the Athenian elite, Alcibiades, provoked by dragging his purple *himation* in the Agora (see Plutarch, *Alcibiades* 16.1). Alcibiades shows off his wealth through his expensive clothing (real purple dye, made using *murex* molluscs, was extremely costly) and his willingness to spoil it. The statement he wishes to make through his behaviour could only be effective if people showed semiotic sensitivity and were able to read what his clothing, and his manipulation of it, symbolised. Everyday life could thus offer experience of the process through which the fifth-century theatre audience was able to establish information about tragic characters from their costumes; it is the same process at work in both cases. We have a glimpse of this process – that is, of how the audience responded to costume and deduced information from its semiotic coding – from within the plays themselves. Certain characters, both in tragedy and comedy, act as internal spectators, responding to what they see on stage, and present a mirror image of the audience's experience of viewing and reading costume. In these self-reflexive moments, one character explicitly comments on the outfit of another and vocalises the thought process in trying to decode it; this offers an internalised representation of the spectator's response to costume.

A simple example of this is offered in Euripides' *Hecuba* 733-5, where Agamemnon on first spotting the corpse of Polydorus comments as follows (tr. Collard 1991):

> Ha! What man is this I see dead beside the tents? A Trojan, for
> the clothes which wrap his body tell me he is no Argive.

Agamemnon is confronted by the visual information of a wrapped corpse and immediately engages in a process of interpretation. He answers his own question of what he is looking at, by using the clues that are offered by the costume. He infers that the corpse is Trojan and not Greek from the type of cloth used to wrap it. He vocalises the process of reading costume in which the audience silently engages when watching a play. Even more strikingly, his lines confirm that it was quite natural in ancient Greek thought to think about costume as the bearer of information, i.e. the equivalent to a sign; since the clothing here is conceptualised as capable of communicating information in the same way as a messenger ('tell' is expressed by the Greek verb technically used for a messenger delivering news). These lines are therefore not only helpful in offering a reflection of the audience's process of interpreting costume, but they provide an insight into how costume was understood to be a silent visual communicator. The fundamental concepts of semiotics were, therefore, not only in operation in performance, but also a part of the way in which the original audience consciously thought about tragedy.

A more complex example of such a moment in tragedy is offered by Aeschylus' *Suppliants*, in which the Argive king, Pelasgus, is faced with a group of female suppliants who are demanding his help. His first priority is to try to establish who these women are (in fact, they are the daughters of Danaus, who have fled from Egypt to escape marriage with their cousins, the sons of Aegyptus) and he does this through looking at their outfits (Aeschylus, *Suppliants* 234-53, tr. Sommerstein 2009):

> **Pelasgus** From what place does this company come that I am addressing, in un-Greek garb, wearing luxurious barbarian robes and headbands? The dress of these women is not from the Argive region, nor from any place in Greece. And how you dared to come to this land so fearlessly, under the protection neither of heralds nor of native sponsors, and without guides – that is astonishing. And yet suppliant-branches are lying beside you, before the Assembled Gods, in accordance with our customs: only in that respect would 'Greece' be a reasonable guess. About other things, too, it would be proper to make many more conjectures, if there were not a person here with a voice to explain to me.
>
> **Chorus** What you have said about our attire is perfectly true; but how should I address *you* – as a private individual, or a temple warden carrying a sacred staff, or the leader of the city?
>
> **Pelasgus** So far as that is concerned, you can answer and speak to me with confidence. I am Pelasgus, ruler of this city, son of earth-born Palaechthon; and this land is cultivated by the race of the Pelasgians, appropriately named after me their king.

The king tries to interpret the clues offered by what the women are wearing. He vocalises his thought process as he responds to the visual data and tries to analyse its symbolism. First, he notices that the clothing is not Greek and from this answers one of the first critical questions that an ancient theatre spectator must ask: where is the character from? Are they Greek or not? He deduces from their style of clothing that they must have

48

come from outside Greece. Next he sees the prop which is a crucial part of their costume: the suppliant's branch. This sign is much easier for him, or as he implies for any Greek, to interpret since it was established in the semiotic system of everyday life in their society. He can therefore know instantly from the branches that this group are asking for protection in the name of the gods. So far the king's response to the women's costume must echo the process which the audience had already gone through at the chorus' first entrance. As the audience identify with the king's process of deduction and thinking, they must become aware of their own engagement in that process of semiotic analysis (reading the costume); that is, for a moment they become aware of the use of encoding and decoding in the theatrical performance.

This self-consciousness about the semiotic process is heightened further by the final line of the king's opening speech where he draws attention to the limitations of that system of communication and the dependence of theatre on the interplay between words and spectacle (and between verbal and visual languages.) What he suggests is that he could not know the rest of their story, except by guesswork, were the women not there to answer his questions. In this, he acknowledges the limitations of costume as a theatrical sign – he can learn only a limited amount from it and for the rest he will have to depend on words. What limits the costume is that it can mean something only to those who know the code or language. King Pelasgus' semiotic competence only allows him to deduce that they are foreign and that they are suppliants, anything beyond this is guesswork. In order to understand the costumes further, he needs some instruction and direction. The chorus' answers will teach him that these 'luxurious barbarian robes' are, in fact, Egyptian. This too reflects the experience of the theatre audience, since they may only interpret costume according to their existing knowledge of the semiotic code, and to this end it is some- times necessary for playwrights to offer further verbal direction (through the words of the characters) on how to interpret a costume (see below). The implicit point that the king makes about the limitations of a semiotic system is reinforced by the women's question to the king about his status. They are evidently unable to determine the answer from what he is wearing. They can make guesses about what his sceptre might signify, but they can only *know* which guess is right from his reply; they do not have sufficient knowledge of the language of Greek costume to be able to deduce it for themselves. So this immediately offers an illustration of the king's implicit claim that a theatrical sign's potential to communicate or to mean something is dependent on the spectator's knowledge of the semiotic code and, failing that, on verbal confirmation. The audience, in contrast to the women, are presumably able to identify Pelasgus' role at his first entry, since they have a better knowledge of the semiotic conventions for repre- senting a king in tragedy. The audience's awareness of the contrast between their ability to understand the costume and the chorus' inability draws their attention back to the process of semiotic analysis and invites reflection on what makes the difference between the successful interpretation of a costume and drawing a blank.

There is also engagement with the semiotic process of reading costumes in ancient comedy, often to humorous effect. So, for example, in Aristophanes' *Women at the Thesmophoria* 141-4, the character Inlaw expresses his confusion in trying to interpret the effeminate character Agathon's appearance (tr. Sommerstein 1994):

> And what about yourself, young 'un? Have you been reared a man? Then where's your prick? Where's your cloak? Where are your Laconian shoes? Or as a woman, was it? Then where are your tits? What's your answer? Why aren't you saying anything?

In this scene, the question of how to read a costume is again at stake. In fact, earlier in the passage (at line 136), Aristophanes has signalled to the audience that he is about to engage with this issue, by making Inlaw quote a line from an Aeschylean play in which a character tries to establish another's identity from his costume. There is, of course, a difference in the effect that the questioning has in tragedy and comedy; presumably Inlaw's interrogation caused laughter, while its tragic counterpart invited quiet reflection. And yet, at the same time, this kind of character interaction may in one sense produce a similar audience response regardless of whether it is in tragedy or comedy. Inlaw's approach may be humorously direct and vulgar, but it potentially mirrors the audience's own response and thought process in the same way as Pelasgus' speech had. The audience may too have been at a loss as to how to interpret Agathon's appearance, and the vocalisation of that confusion, which they have felt, again heightens their awareness of the necessary semiotic process of reading costume in theatre and the potential challenges of this. The joke is that Agathon was a 'real' character, in that he was a tragic playwright in ancient Athens and known in real life. The audience, therefore, cannot really be at a loss over how to categorise him, and yet imagining him as a semiotic prospect for someone like Inlaw, who did not know him, demonstrates just how unstable his outward appearance made his gender identity. On the dialectic between gender identity and theatre in this passage, see the excellent analysis by Duncan (2006, 25-57).

Beneath the humour of this and the chance to poke fun at Agathon, Aristophanes is able to invite the audience to reflect in a serious way on some of the fundamentals of costume and therefore theatre. Inlaw, like Pelasgus, recognises that when he reaches the limits of his own ability to interpret visual information, or theatrical signs, he has to fall back on words and interrogation. Aristophanes acknowledges implicitly through this that costume sometimes depends on further verbal comment and direction from characters within the play in order to clarify their intended semiotic meaning.

These passages point to an essential principle behind the creation of costume's meaning on the fifth-century stage: it comes through the partnership of the visual (the actual costume) and the verbal. The words spoken in the play were a fundamental means through which to activate specific meanings to the costumes presented in a fifth-century production. The way in which a costume is described either by the character wearing it, or by another character, could alter the audience's perception of what it meant. These comments do not always occur in the contexts which we have been looking at, where the meaning of the costume is explicitly at stake, but often characters offer a description of their costume where its full meaning is not self-explanatory from its visual appearance alone. In this sense, descriptions of costume may add not only clarity to its meaning, resolving any kind of ambiguity, but also depth to its symbolism, since it can enable the costume to have a far more specific meaning. So, for example, in Aeschylus' *Persians*, the Persian King Xerxes returns from being defeated by the Greeks and is presented wearing tattered clothing. The audience would have been able to read this costume as representative of his suffering, but the semiotic potential of the costume and the *pathos* that it is able to generate are heightened by the comments made about it by Darius and by Xerxes himself. Darius, Xerxes' father, comments on it even before Xerxes appears on stage, warning the chorus that Xerxes' fine clothing, which he wore on his departure, has now been shredded in tatters through grief (Aeschylus, *Persians* 835-6). This information given within the play to the chorus, in fact, offers direction to the audience for how they should understand the costume when it appears. This offers an example of where verbal direction is given to the audience in advance of the costume's appearance on stage so that its meaning will be immediately apparent. The symbolism is then reinforced by Xerxes himself, at line 1030, who draws attention to his clothing and explains its state to the chorus; the impact of his comment is all the stronger because it is made about a costume while it is visible to the audience. The verbal comments add depth to the symbolism of the costume, since the knowledge that this was the finery that Xerxes had worn on the way out to battle, enables his tattered clothing to become a visual symbol for the complete change in fortune that the Persians have suffered.

Elsewhere, characters comment on their own costumes in a way that puts emphasis on an already evident meaning; so, for example, Electra in Euripides' *Electra* 185 comments on the poor state of her clothing and her poverty, while Hermione in Euripides' *Andromache* 147-8 comments on the finest of her clothing and her high status. These comments may confirm the audience's first impression of the costumes and enhance the perception of their fabric as either particularly poor or fine. At the same time, each comment also acts in an analogous way to a camera zoom in film and draws attention to the costume, emphasizing the aspect of the character's state that it represents. In fifth-century productions, performed in open-air theatres, verbal comments took the place of lighting as the means through which to direct the audience's attention to some specific element of what was being presented on stage. So comments such as these had the dual purpose of inviting audience attention onto the costume and while they focussed on it, changing or enhancing their reading of it. The verbal comments also offer an opportunity to create meaning through costume in a more indirect way, since the comments are not only significant to an understanding of the costume, but also of the character who makes them. A character's perception of a costume may manipulate the audience's reading of it, but at the same time it may also reveal something about them as a character. If we think back to the example of Hermione and Electra, then their comments on their own costumes offer clues to characterisation. Both characters are presented as particularly self-conscious through the comments that they make and in addition to this, Electra comes across as self-pitying and Hermione as proud. We will look more fully at the theatrical impact that could be created by the use of verbal commentary on costumes in the next chapter.

Verbal comment is not the only way of putting emphasis on costume or changing the audience's perception of its meaning. 'Movement' could also create possibilities of directing audience attention to the costume or inviting them to see it in a new way. This 'movement' covers both the idea of physical manipulation of the costume and also the entrance or exit of characters; both could affect perception of its meaning. The first, physical manipulation, might involve the rearrangement of the costume or a removal of a part of it. Either action alters the actual appearance of the material object and potentially its symbolism too. In Euripides' *Heracles* 1159, for example, Heracles (who has just discovered that he has killed his wife and children in a fit of god-sent madness) will rearrange his cloak (*himation*) by drawing it up over his head so that he is veiled by it. The material objects making up the costume have remained the same, but by rearranging the *himation* Heracles has changed its symbolic meaning so that in this reconfiguration it expresses and represents his shame. The audience's perception of what the costume means has been altered by its rearrangement. In Aeschylus' *Agamemnon* 1264-8, Cassandra throws down her prophetess's insignia; this removal of a part of her costume reconfigures it and invites the audience to reassess its meaning (see further below and Chapter 4). The other type of movement, the entrance or exit of characters, works in a more subtle way by changing the audience's perception of costumes. It is by contrast that the entrance of a character may throw a new light on the costumes of characters already on stage. So, for example, in Euripides' *Electra*, the poor state of Electra's clothing must strike the audience anew when the well-dressed Orestes enters (at line 82). Similarly the entrance of the Argive king in Aeschylus'

3. Semiotics and the Language of Tragic Costume

Suppliants (at line 234) and the visual contrast his appearance offers, must put emphasis on the 'foreignness' of the daughters of Danaus. So, that even before the king gives his verbal commentary on their appearance, the audience is already thinking about that difference and the women's ethnicity. The appearance of the herald (line 873f.), spokesman for the sons of Aegyptus, also dressed in a way to show that they are from Egypt, will have a different impact on the perception of these women's costumes, again. The entrance or exit of characters may in this way accent certain qualities of the costumes already on stage and this refocus can then be played on further, by verbal comments.

So far, the discussion about the nature of tragic costume and the way of reading it could be applied equally to tragedy or comedy, but there is something specific to the semiotics of tragic costume which must be taken into account by anyone hoping to reconstruct the ancient experience of decoding it. One of the differences between tragic and comic costume is that tragic costume relies entirely on clothing or accessories, and of course, the mask, in order to represent a character. This difference becomes most obvious in the ways in which the two genres suggest the gender of a character. The Choregoi vase (Fig. 11), juxtaposes the two approaches: on the right the three characters in comic costume each have the leather *phallus* hanging down, making their gender beyond doubt, while the tragic-costumed Aegisthus on the left has nothing of the sort from which to determine his gender. It is exactly this difference between tragic and comic costume which makes it so difficult for Inlaw in Aristophanes' *Women at the Thesmophoria* (see above) to read Agathon's costume, since there is no outward physical sign of his gender visible (on the *phallus* in comedy see Stone 1980, 72-126). Related to this is the observation that in tragedy, unlike in comedy, the audience is not encouraged to think about the body of the actor beneath the costume, rather it is everything seen on the surface which represents the character, see Foley (2000). The implication of this is that the tragic character could continue to exist after the performance of a play, embodied in the costume he or she had been presented in. Precisely this idea is exploited to comic effect by Aristophanes in his *Acharnians* 393-489, where characters from Euripides' tragedies are understood to continue to exist in the costumes which remain from the productions (see Chapter 4).

Once we have noted this difference, it becomes clear that in order to enjoy tragic theatre, the audience had to be able to accept that the costume (*skeue* – clothing, props and mask) makes up the whole of the represented character's being. The reading of clothing in everyday life could not actually prepare the audience to accept this particular quality of tragic semiotics, since in real life clothing may represent a temporary social role, identity or *persona*, but the individual's outfit is not understood to be the sum total of his or her being. So how was it that the ancient audience could make the leap to being able to understand and accept a costume as representative of a person's entire entity? The answer seems to lie with Dionysus, the god of drama. The general question of the role which Dionysian ritual played in the origin of tragedy is still controversial with both its advocates and its sceptics (see Scullion 2002; Csapo and Miller 2007). But the point here is a more specific one about the impact that the worship of Dionysus, as a cultural experience, had on society's range of modes for reading clothing. In effect, it seems to me that the semiotic conceptualisation of Dionysus in the sixth and fifth centuries BC facilitated and then supported the audience's understanding of tragic costume as representative of an entire stage identity. The visual evidence from this period reveals that in the cultural imagination, Dionysus had a special connection with cloth and clothing. Exceptionally for a god in this period, he is usually depicted clothed and, even more strikingly, could be represented in ritual by a pole draped in a cloth with a mask at its top (see Osborne 1997). In the ritual scenario, then, the spectators gained experience of perceiving a set of clothing and mask as representative of an entire being (the pole is merely the support and the identity comes from the clothing and mask). It is the experience of this semiotic conceptualisation of the god which, arguably, conditioned late sixth- and fifth-century theatre spectators to accept tragic costume as representative of an entire stage character. The ritual offers the spectators experience of viewing in the way demanded by theatre (on this idea see further Wyles 2007, 54-6). The nature of tragic costume was perhaps even determined by this ritual experience; it was certainly able to emerge in the way that it did thanks to the mode of representing the god and the impact this had on cultural perceptions of clothing's semiotic capabilities. The implications of tragic costume being so independent of the body (and therefore actor) and solely representative of the character will be explored in the next chapter.

This point about Dionysus leads on to a more important one about the origins of theatre costume in general. Since theatre costume is a sign and its meaning is constructed through the semiotic processes of encoding and decoding, its material design is not what is at stake when searching for origins; i.e. it is not about hunting for the original garment that tragic costume was based on (see p. 80; in any case, as Chapter 1 shows, there is not 'a' design for tragic costume in the fifth century, least of all at the beginning of it). In terms of the development of theatre costume, and even theatre in general, it is far more productive to think about the cultural coding and ways of viewing which allowed the semiotic process, essential to reading a tragic costume, to emerge. The cultural experience of the representation of Dionysus in ritual was not the only one to be important to the emergence of tragic costume. Other aspects of Dionysian ritual are relevant too, such as the use of the mask by the worshippers – important not so much because of the loss of identity for the participant (as has been claimed) but for the construction of an identity as seen by the viewer. Equally, other rituals involving different types of dressing up had a part to play as a foundation for the ability to understand the semiotic processes inherent in theatre costume; important here are the vases showing men dressed up as animal choruses (see Green 1985), and the evidence for ritual disguise (see Lada Richards 1999, 330-6). Beyond ritual, the language of tragic costume also owed its foundation to modes of viewing and visual codes from everyday society, art, and poetry. The everyday offered a foundation to the audience both in knowing how to read clothing and in understanding what specific symbols meant. The basic building blocks of the language must have depended on pre-existing codes from the everyday which could allow the playwright to represent (among other things): luxury, poverty, suffering, or grief. Also strongly gendered items of clothing from everyday life could be brought onto the stage in order to offer a means, other than the differentiation in the shade of the mask, through which to communicate the sex of a character. The way of suggesting a male character through costume is nicely reflected in Aristophanes' *Assembly Women* where the women disguise themselves as men by putting on beards, cloaks, and Laconian shoes, and walking with sticks (and Inlaw, in the passage from Aristophanes' *Women at the Thesmophoria* quoted above, tellingly looks for a Laconian shoe in his attempt to determine Agathon's gender).

Representational art and poetry (especially Homer) could be helpful to the playwright and audience, for the pre-existing symbolism which they gave to certain items and also for the way of reading clothing suggested by these. While the everyday could provide symbols for general human conditions, gender, or social status, art and poetry offered the symbols through which to identify the gods and specific characters in the body of myth. Through the iconographic traditions of art and the poetic traditions of lyric and epic, it would be easy for the audience to identify certain figures on the stage: Heracles through his lion skin, bow, and club, Athena by her *aegis*, Hermes by his *caduceus* (wand) and winged sandals, etc. In this sense, art and poetry provided the playwright with the building blocks for the language of tragic costume. The idea that theatre borrowed its costumes from Homer is hinted at by Aristophanes in his *Wasps* (351), where the chorus suggest to the comic hero Philocleon that he could make his escape by dressing in rags like wily Odysseus. The comment suggests that the Homeric epics offered theatre a wardrobe of possible costumes; Philocleon could take a disguise from the epic model, just as the playwright could.

In a more fundamental sense, both art and poetry were also important to the development of theatre costume through the way in which they trained society to view. Art relied on a visual code and on the viewer being able to decode its symbols in order to determine what the picture was showing. Sometimes there might be an inscription on the vase to give the viewer a clue as to the identity of the characters shown there, but if not then it was up to the viewer to work it out from the set of visual information and the context in which it was framed. In theatre, of course, as we have seen, there was the possibility of supplementing the visual with the verbal in order to clarify the encoded meaning of costume, but the initial assessment by the audience of a character's identity must have followed a process very like the one which they had already experienced in viewing vases, wall paintings, etc. Poetry, and especially Homer, offers a different kind of groundwork and training for the successful comprehension of theatre costume. First, Homer encourages his audience to understand a character's identity through specific qualities, which are expressed in stock-epithets such as 'swift-footed Achilles' and 'rosy-fingered Dawn'. These character-identifying epithets often have a material part and are embodied in items of clothing. So, for example, characteristic of Hector is his shiny helmet: he is described as Hector 'of the flashing helm' (*koruthaiolos*). The helmet functions within the poem in the same way as a prop could on stage; so that Hector's identity and role is defined by the helmet he wears. In the moment where he is presented playing the role of father instead of warrior, he is in fact made to remove his helmet: this occurs in the well-known scene where the baby Astyanax is frightened by the helmet (*Iliad* 6.466-94). When Hector leaves to return to the battlefield he assumes his identity as warrior once more by putting his helmet back on. Homer plays with the material counterpart to Hector's epithet 'of the flashing-helm' (*koruthaiolos*) in this scene and explores how this portable symbol of identity when taken off or put back may communicate a character-role. It is clear from this that Homeric epic, as much as Dionysian ritual and art, had a part to play in preparing to see items of clothing as symbolic of character identity. Equally Odysseus, as already mentioned, offered an easy model for theatre costume and the principle of 'dressing up in imitation' in his use of disguise in the *Odyssey* (see Muecke 1982a), and similarly Patroclus dressing up as Achilles by wearing his armour in the *Iliad* offers a model for the transformative power of costume (explored in Chapter 4).

But going beyond the construction of identity or a stage-character's presence through costume to the actual use of costume during a performance, Homer also had something to offer the playwright here. Hector's helmet has already provided one example of how Homer explores and exploits the use of symbolic gesture with clothing and the impact it has on the perception of a character's identity: Hector removes the helmet and momentarily discards, or sidelines, his role as a warrior. Andromache, fainting and losing the veil given to her on her wedding day, assumes her new role as widow (*Iliad* 22.462-72; see below). Cassandra in Aeschylus' *Agammemnon* 1264-8 attempts to exploit this principle, when by throwing down her prophetess's insignia, she tries to forsake her role as prophetess (see Chapter 4). Homer can be argued to be the ultimate source for the audience's understanding of this kind of symbolic gesture. The symbolic manipulation of props in Homer's poetry offers the basis for a similar

56

usage on stage and a model for semiotics. Achilles throws down the sacred sceptre to lay emphasis on the oath he has spoken. The action is made effective because Achilles has carefully encoded this object with meaning by the description he offers of it, and as a result the gesture of throwing it down takes on full significance (*Iliad* 1.233-46, tr. Lattimore 1961):

'But I will tell you this and swear a great oath upon it:
in the name of this sceptre, which never again will bear leaf nor
branch, now that it has left behind the cut stump in the mountains,
nor shall it ever blossom again, since the bronze blade stripped
bark and leafage, and now at last the sons of the Achaians
carry it in their hands in state when they administer
the justice of Zeus. And this shall be a great oath before you:
some day longing for Achilleus will come to the sons of the Achaians,
all of them. Then stricken at heart though you be, you will be able
to do nothing, when in their numbers before man-slaughtering Hektor
they drop and die. And then you will eat out the heart within you
in sorrow, that you did no honour to the best of the Achaians.'
Thus spoke Peleus' son and dashed to the ground the sceptre
studded with golden nails, and sat down again.

Without Achilles' description of the sceptre, his action could not have the same impact either on his immediate audience or on the audience of the poem. Similarly the symbolism of the veil of Andromache falling from her head can only be understood fully by the audience because of the description of it which accompanies the report of the action; (*Iliad* 22.462-72, tr. Lattimore 1961):

But when she came to the bastion and where the men were gathered
she stopped, staring, on the wall; and she saw him
being dragged in front of the city, and the running horses
dragged him at random toward the hollow ships of the Achaians.
The darkness of night misted over the eyes of Andromache.
She fell backward, and gasped the life breath from her, and far off
threw from her head the shining gear that ordered her headdress,
the diadem and the cap, and the holding-band woven together,
and the circlet, which Aphrodite the golden once had given her
on that day when Hektor of the shining helmet led her forth
from the house of Eëtion, and gave numberless gifts to win her.

This technique of encoding objects with meaning through description is the equivalent of the playwright's use of verbal comment to construct or enhance the meaning of costume which we have already seen. Achilles' very deliberate description of the sceptre operates in the same way as a character's self-conscious comment on an element of his/her own costume, while the additional, and symbolically crucial, information about Andromache's circlet offered in the narrative, has the equivalent function to a comment made by another character. Through passages like these,

Homer offers a framework for the interplay between the material object (the sign) and the words which describe it and direct the interpretation of its meaning. He also shows how to invest a gesture, involving this item, with a particular symbolic force through exploitation of this interplay. This kind of combined usage of items, descriptions, and actions, is not possible in plastic art which represents a static moment and has no opportunity to 'explain' the before or after, but is of course possible in theatre. In this sense Homer's contribution to the language of tragic costume and the audience's appreciation of its manipulation in perform-ance are fundamental.

While Homer could offer the foundations for the playwright's encoding and the audience's decoding of symbolic items of costume in the play, the language of tragic costume would gradually develop its own layers of meaning for costume and range of ways to exploit it on stage. Each tragic playwright contributed to the nature of the language of costume, through the way in which he chose to handle it and the meanings which he created for individual items of costume. The language of costume, what costume meant, and how it was used, were not fixed during the fifth century, any more than its material objects were (see Chapter 1). Instead the language was organic and developing its possibilities, vocabulary, and range with each performance. Within this system of development and expansion, it was possible for meanings to be generated through allusion to the usage and symbolism of costume in past productions. This principle of a play exploiting performance history in order to create meaning is explored by the theatre scholar Carlson who discusses it in terms of subsequent productions being 'haunted' by what had gone before (see Carlson 1994a, 1994b). Following this principle, a particularly iconic use of a piece of costume by a tragedian could be alluded to and exploited in order to create meaning in subsequent plays.

One example of such an iconic use might be the sword in Sophocles' *Ajax* which plays a central role – it is the instrument of the tragic hero's suicide, and before the fatal act Ajax makes a speech addressed to it (lines 815f.). The striking focus on the sword in this play makes it possible for tragedi-ans to refer back to it (and everything it stands for in the *Ajax*), by the shorthand of a visual or verbal allusion in subsequent productions. This kind of inter-performative allusion to a previous handling of a piece of costume may be used in the same way as a literary allusion within a poem to create meaning by showing similarity or difference, or by suggesting a certain context for interpretation. Sophocles' treatment of the sword in the *Ajax* adds a layer of meaning (with a whole cluster of symbolic associa-tions) to the sword, as a unit in the language of costume. This layer may be brought to the surface, even if momentarily, by an allusion, or covered over with new meanings in subsequent productions. So, the language of costume in the fifth century was made up of a collection of pieces of costume, the meanings of which were being built on, altered, and nuanced with each performance. As the layers of meanings from past performances multiplied, the potential depth of each object's symbolism grew and the language of tragic costume could gradually become more sophisticated (employing, for example, subtext through inter-performative allusions). The independent journey and development in meaning of each piece of costume through different productions can be described as its 'stage life' (see Sofer 2003).

The possibility of exploiting the past symbolic usage of costume in a production depends on the audience's performance memory. In other words, the audience have to be familiar with the past theatrical moment which is being alluded to, in order for the allusion to be effective. It is for this reason that it seems likely that only iconic uses of costume, and the layers of meaning they created, would be alluded to and exploited by tragedians. Even so, the particular framework for theatrical productions offered a clear advantage to fifth-century playwrights in terms of deliberate 'haunting' and exploitation of past performances. Since the Great Dionysia festival took place just once a year and offered only one performance of each play, the audience, in any given year, all shared the same theatrical experience. In contrast, modern theatre-going is far more disparate in the sense that there is usually a run of performance so that even if two people have seen the same production, their experience of it could be significantly different depending on which night they attended. The Athenian system created an audience with a very strong performance memory, as the parodies of tragedy in comic productions demonstrate. There is an explicit allusion to the audience's process of remembering previous performances in Aristophanes' *Women at the Thesmophoria* 1060-1. In this part of the comedy, Aristophanes is parodying a tragedy called *Andromeda* which had been produced the year before. In the parody, Euripides, who is a character in the comedy and is here playing the part of Echo (who had been a character in *Andromeda*), prompts the audience to recognise him by reminding them that he had been performing in the same place the year before. The continuity of the place of performance must have facilitated the kind of visual allusion and memory prompting which was essential to being able to exploit the symbolism of past productions. The comment made by Echo suggests that there was at least a portion of the audience who could be assumed to have attended the year before (or at least have knowledge of the tragic performance from that year). The astonishing strength of performance memory of the audience at the Dionysia is suggested by Aristophanes' *Acharnians*. In this comedy, Aristophanes again alludes to a tragedy by Euripides and depends on the audience remembering that play in order for them to find his comedy humorous. But this time Aristophanes chooses Euripides' *Telephus*, which had been produced thirteen years before! Aristophanes could clearly depend on the audience's performance memory, if he was going to risk alluding to a play from such a long time before. The specific circumstances of theatrical performances in Athens which produced an audience with such a strong performance memory left the possibilities of exploiting the theatrical past wide open and this must explain why the fifth century proved to be such a fertile period for the development of theatre in general and the language of tragic costume in particular. Tragedians could employ costume in a semiotically-complex way because they could rely on the audience being well-versed in past usage and, therefore, being familiar with the language and able to understand what was being communicated.

This chapter has explored the idea of how the significance of tragic costume in a play depended on more than its material design. It is clear from the passages that we have looked at from tragedy and comedy, which mirror the audience's experience of reading tragic costume, that costume was treated as a theatrical sign within the performance, something with a meaning to be interpreted in order to heighten an appreciation of the play. Costume is encoded with a meaning which the audience are interested to decode. Both processes, of encoding and decoding, may depend on the interplay between the spectacle and the words, the visual and the verbal. So while a piece of costume might mean something to the audience even before anything is said about it, often verbal commentary might direct or enhance the audience's understanding of it and add further specific layers to its symbolism. The system of the language of costume and the audience's ability to read tragic costume owes something to ritual, the everyday, art and poetry (especially Homer). These should be recognised as the significant 'origins' of tragic costume rather than any specific garment. Since costume was more than a material thing, each playwright's contribution to costume was not a question of whether they introduced sleeves or boots, as some of the ancient sources suggest (see Appendix), but rather is found in how his handling of costume expanded its semiotic potential. Over the fifth century the language of costume, and its sophistication, could evolve through the multiplying of layers of meaning (embedded in each piece of costume) and the emergence of a theatrical past which the playwright could exploit in his costuming strategy. Since so many plays are lost to us we cannot know the full range of semiotic effects produced by each playwright, but in the next chapter we will look at what we can establish about the language of costume by analysing it 'in action' in the surviving plays.

Costume in Action

The last chapter explored the idea of costume as something more than a material object – as a theatrical sign to be interpreted. Costume, as a sign, operates within the structure of what I have referred to as the language of costume. The audience engage in a semiotic process when they interpret a costume; they use their knowledge of the language of costume to decode it and determine its meaning. The meaning of a costume, or the audience's perception of it, may alter during a performance as new readings of it are suggested through verbal comment, inter-performative allusion, physical manipulation, or visual contrast. In this chapter, we will see those principles in action and examine the way in which costume was used to create meaning and dramatic effect in fifth-century tragedies. The discussion explores this through focusing on six major aspects of the language of costume: identity, determinism, emotional manipulation, ethnicity, the historical dimension, and fabrication.

I. Identity

The construction of identity is one of the most fundamental functions of costume. The process of putting on clothing in order to construct a character is, in fact, essential to the creation of theatre. We have already discussed, in the previous chapter, the roots of the conceptual thinking that allowed the audience to accept a set of clothing as representative of a character and symbolic of their identity. In this section, we will look at the dramatic potential of that acceptance and how the playwright could exploit the status of items of costume as absolutely representative of a character's identity.

The ancient audience's understanding of the relationship between theatre costume and stage identity is reflected in, and simultaneously informed by, Aristophanes' comedies. One of the questions which Aristophanes is interested to explore in his plays is centred on the processes behind the creation of a theatrical event. Often the action of his comedies leads the audience back-stage – if not literally, then at least in their imagination. So, for example, the comment by one of his heroes in *Peace* 174, about the handling of the *mechane* (crane) invites the audience to think about what is going on 'behind the scenes' in order to produce this stage effect. It is not surprising therefore to find a representation of dressing up in costume taking place on stage in Aristophanes' plays. This too is a means of reflecting on the process of creating theatre. We have already touched on some of the examples from his comedies where men dress up as women (*Women at the Thesmophoria*) or where women dress up as men (*Assembly Women*). Both of these as acts of dressing up in disguise, are closely analogous to the actor's process of putting on theatre costume and therefore may reflect on it (see Muecke 1982b). But there is a limit to the analogy since getting dressed up as 'a woman' (which is general) is not the same as getting dressed up as a *particular* character. There is an example, however, from another Aristophanic comedy where the act of putting on a theatre costume in order to become a named character is directly and explicitly represented on stage. The scene is found in *Acharnians* 393-489 where the comic hero Dicaeopolis goes to Euripides' house with the intention of borrowing the tragic costume of Telephus (a character from one of his plays), from him. The following extract is the part of the scene where Euripides hands over the costume and Dicaeopolis puts it on (*Acharnians* 433-49, tr. Sommerstein 1973):

> **Eur.** Give to him, slave, the rags of Telephus. They lie above Thyestes', and below poor Ino's robe.
> **Slave** Here, catch.
> **Dic.** 'O Zeus who seest through and under all!' – Euripides, since you have been so kind, could you possibly give me the things that go with the outfit? The Mysian cloth cap, for example?
> 'For I this day must seem to be a beggar –
> Be who I am, but not appear myself.'
> Or to be more accurate – the audience have got to know who I am, but the Chorus have got to be fooled, at least until my telling Telephean phrases have knocked them into the middle of next week.
> **Eur.** I'll give it thee: for subtle are thy schemes, and intricate the courses of thy mind.
> **Dic.** 'Oh be thou blest; and as for Telephus
> Thou knowest what I wish as touching him.'
> Dear me! you're making me quite poetic already. Now – I still need a stick, if I'm to be a proper beggar.
> **Eur.** Take this, and quit thou straight these marble halls.

This encounter reveals just how closely connected costume and character identity were in fifth-century theatre. Dicaeopolis asks to borrow the costume of a tragic character, Telephus, who was remembered from Euripides' *Telephus* for his ragged appearance and his skill at making speeches. This background is relevant to the reasons for *this* character's costume being chosen by Dicaeopolis, and ultimately, by Aristophanes, when in fact there was a whole catalogue of rag costumes belonging to tragic heroes (listed just before the passage quoted above) from which a costume could have been chosen. The choice of Telephus is not coincidental and serves two purposes. First, it fits Dicaeopolis' requirements since he, like Telephus, will have to make a defence speech in a tricky situation and therefore he hopes that *this* costume will help him to succeed in the task. It also works well with Aristophanes' intent to use this scene to comment on theatre costume and how it functions. Telephus' costume makes an excellent choice for this second purpose, since in the Euripidean play the rags had been a piece of disguise and they therefore already had the potential in this original context to invite reflection on theatre costume (see above). Aristophanes responds to this potential and develops it by making it even more obvious to the audience: instead of using the rags disguise as a metaphor for theatre costume (as Euripides seems to have), in the comedy the rags which Dicaeopolis borrows are explicitly referred to as theatre costume; the figurative becomes literal and the theatrically-reflexive comment is made more direct. So what is the comment that Aristophanes makes and what does he show us in this scene about the relationship between costume and identity?

The effect on Dicaeopolis of putting on Telephus' costume demonstrates the closeness of the connection between costume and identity in ancient Greek theatre. Dicaeopolis comments explicitly on the effect of the costume (line 447): 'Dear me! you're making me quite poetic already.' The Greek carries the idea that the clothing is literally 'filling him' with lines of poetry; the audience have already seen this for themselves since all of a sudden this comic hero is quoting lines from tragedy. The idea here, then, is that as soon as Dicaeopolis puts on the costume of Telephus, he begins to speak like that character. Furthermore, he also starts behaving like him as he plays the beggar, pestering Euripides and asking for more and more props until he is sent away (see Muecke 1982a). So this costume, belonging to a character who had been presented on the stage thirteen years earlier, is still capable of conjuring his stage presence and may even impose the character's qualities, behavioural traits and way of speaking, on whoever puts it on. That is not to say, of course, that the fifth-century audience believed that the clothing had a magical power to transform the wearer, but they were clearly able to accept this conceptual way of thinking about the process of an actor 'becoming' a character. The concept that it is somehow all down to the costume is nicely brought out by the krater in Boston showing two chorusmen (Fig. 5): one is fully dressed and so is already in character as a choruswoman, while the other is still not quite dressed and therefore is not yet in role. Similarly on the Pronomos vase (Fig. 9) it is only the satyr who is wearing all of his costume, i.e. with his mask on as well, who dances as though in role.

All this adds up to the idea that 'becoming' a character depends on putting on costume. The implication of this is that the whole of a charac-ter's identity was bound up in the costume so that there was an almost complete identification of a character with the material of his or her semiotic representation. As a result of this a character could be understood to continue to exist, even after the end of a performance, 'frozen' in the

costume. If it were then put into storage (either literally or in the performance memory of the audience), then the character could be reanimated in
later performances whenever anyone else put on the costume. This is a
striking and quite unique (at least compared with most modern productions in the Western tradition) aspect to costume in ancient theatre. The
limiting factor which prevents the same kind of reanimation in modern
theatre is that performances are mostly unmasked. This means that a
costume which becomes iconic and associated in the cultural imagination
with a particular stage character can never have the same autonomy from
the actor as the ancient costume. If we think of Eliza Doolittle in *My Fair
Lady* and her iconic black and white striped costume, which she wears for
the races, then we also think of Audrey Hepburn who played that character. In other words, the costume is associated both with the character Eliza
Doolittle and the actress Audrey Hepburn. In ancient theatre, where
masks were used, this does not happen, and that enables the costume to
belong exclusively to a character. This opens up the possibility of the kind
of reanimation that we have just looked at, but the closeness of identification between character identity and costume also offers other opportu-
nities to the playwright.

Aristophanes exploits this close association between character and
costume to comic effect in another of his plays. In his *Frogs*, the character
Dionysus depends on the fact that costume works on the same principle as
illustrated in the scene from *Acharnians* discussed above. Relying on this
principle (though not explicitly), Dionysus assumes that putting on the
iconic pieces of Heracles' costume will somehow give him that hero's
qualities of courage and enable him to complete the equivalent feats; just
as Dicaeopolis assumes, and is shown to be right in assuming, that if he
can only put on the costume of Telephus then he will become just as
eloquent. In Dionysus' case, however, Aristophanes pushes the limits of
costume's ability to represent character and shows how it might fail.
Dionysus does not manage to take on the identity of Heracles, or his
qualities, because when confronted with the real Heracles in the play, his
costume looks unconvincing, not least because he has paired up the
Heraclean bits of costume (*skeue*) with an effeminate saffron robe and soft
boots! There is also a sense that the costume cannot, of course, achieve its
purpose in suggesting that Dionysus is Heracles while he is face to face
with the 'real' Heracles. In contrast, the costume is later shown to be
effective when, in the Underworld, Dionysus and then his slave (after a
costume swap) are each mistaken for Heracles with humorous consequences. Even if Aristophanes must primarily be concerned with comic
effects in these scenes, he is also exploring, further establishing and
exploiting this closeness between the physical objects of costume and the
character they represent.

This idea of a costume being so closely bound up with a character's
identity is also found on the tragic stage where the idea of 'identity theft'

through the appropriation of costume is explored. It is treated humorously in Sophocles' *Inachus*, which is now fragmentary but was probably a satyr drama (for a brief discussion and translation of the fragments see Lloyd-Jones 1996, 112-35). Among the fragments is one where Hermes says 'Who is this woman, who has stolen the Arcadian cap?' (fr. 272, tr. Lloyd-Jones 1996). Lloyd-Jones suggests that in this fragment Hermes is addressing Iris. The idea is that Iris appears on stage in an Arcadian cap which Hermes implies really belongs to *him* and *his* costume (after all he was the one who was born in Arcadia). Part of the affront here must be that this supposed theft also carries the suggestion of an attempt to usurp his identity or role. The added humour to the comment comes from the recognition that in fact Iris and Hermes share the same function – since they are both messengers of the gods – and therefore Hermes would have every reason to be nervous about Iris taking his part! Another possible layer to the humour and to the commentary here on how costume operates arises from the recognition that not every appropriation of an atypical piece of costume by a character need necessarily imply an act of identity theft. So, for example, in Sophocles' *Oedipus at Colonus* 313-14, Ismene on her approach is described by Antigone as wearing a Thessalian hat. There is no hint at all here that Ismene is trying to adopt an identity or use the hat as a disguise, rather she is wearing it to protect her from the sun (as Antigone remarks). From this we can infer that it is possible that in the *Inachus*, Iris was wearing the Arcadian cap quite innocently and her action is misread and misrepresented by Hermes, but the punch in the joke comes from the plausibility of the presumption he makes. Hermes' comment depends on the same sense of costume belonging to particular characters and being bound up with their identity which we have already seen in operation in the *Acharnians*. The same idea is exploited again by Sophocles, but in a more serious way, in his *Electra* where Electra complains that Aegisthus is wearing Agamemnon's clothes (lines 267-9). The transfer of costume represents the usurpation of Agamemnon by Aegisthus and his appropriation of his role (see below).

The closeness of the identification between a character and their semiotic representation also has implications for the dramatic impact of the removal of costume. Since costume is so tightly associated with a stage character's identity, removing it can have a striking dramatic effect. In the most extreme cases, this removal or cancelling out of the costume can represent a kind of identity crisis for a character, or even their semiotic death on stage. As an example we might think of Cassandra's stage action, mentioned in the last chapter. She throws down her prophetess' insignia (Aeschylus, *Agamemnon* 1264-72, tr. Lloyd-Jones 1982):

> Why do I preserve these things to mock myself,
> this staff and these fillets of prophecy about my neck?
> You I shall destroy before my death!

Go you to ruin! As you fall, so I pay you back!
Make rich with destruction some other instead of me!
But see, Apollo himself stripping me
of my prophetic raiment, he who has watched me
mightily mocked even with these ornaments upon me
by friends turned enemies, mocked without doubt in vain.

When Cassandra throws down her insignia, she is deconstructing her semiotic representation as a character. The costume had communicated to the audience her identity as prophetess of Apollo; the staff she carries and the fillets she wears inform the audience of this identity. The action on one level represents the 'loss of her primary character trait' (see Griffith 1988). But the semiotic implications of the action go further, since at the same time as removing these bits of costume, she also puts emphasis on her impending death. The audience is therefore invited to read this manipulation of costume as a semiotic prefiguration of the death that is to follow. This is not the loss of a primary character trait so much as a loss of the total sum of the semiotic element of identity – this action represents the 'semiotic death' of a character. Once Cassandra has stripped herself of the parts of her costume, which defined her in semiotic terms, then she has become 'dead' as a stage character. Her mask remains and may continue to identify her, but it offers limited clues to her identity, conveying gender, age, and possibly status, but nothing more of 'who' she is. So this 'semiotic death' plays out in symbolic visual terms the actual death, which she is about to experience off-stage.

Later in the same trilogy it is the addition of a piece of costume which both symbolises and effects transformation. At the conclusion of the *Oresteia*, once Athena has successfully averted the fury of the chorus of Erinyes and they have agreed to live in Athens, the moment is marked by the addition of red cloaks to their costumes. It is in a textually corrupt part of the play (so the context is not completely clear) as Athena commands the escort to accompany the chorus of Erinyes, she says (Aeschylus, *Eumenides* 1028-32, tr. Lloyd-Jones 1982):

> honour them with robes of crimson dye,
> and let the blaze of fire rise up,
> that this their sojourn, kindly to this land,
> may in future time be made manifest in fortune that brings it noble men.

The addition of this piece of costume is a means of enabling the chorus to take on their new role and status as residents of Athens. The significance of its symbolism would be readily obvious to the fifth-century audience, from its visual appearance and the setting in which it is adopted (i.e. as part of a procession), since they were used to seeing *metics* (resident 'outsiders' at Athens) wearing red cloaks for the yearly procession at the Great Panathenaea festival in honour of Athena. Through this costuming, the audience is invited to view the Erinyes as analogous to *metics* (see the note on these lines by Podlecki 1989). This is one of the moments in tragedy where costuming, by echoing contemporary wear, can zoom the action of the play into the present (on this effect see below, on Heracles). Aeschylus exploits the audience's belief in the transformative power of costume, and its character-giving property, in order to give credibility and impact to the stage action. It is not an empty gesture, made only for the sake of making a link with the present, but it is dramatically important for the resolution that it brings. Athena's command is not simply about honouring the Erinyes; in fact she is ensuring that they remain friendly towards Athens by imposing a new role and identity on them through the costume. This act of munificence can therefore also be read as a shrewd manoeuvre through which, by exploiting theatrical principles, to ensure the long-term submission of a city-threatening group. They have been set up as a terrifying force: the Erinyes were apparently so shocking in their scattered entry at the première that they were said to have made children faint and women miscarry (*Life of Aeschylus* 9, tr. in Csapo and Slater 1994, 4.52, p. 260). But by the end of the play they are tamed by the addition of the cloaks which visually cover over their original costumes and semiotically impose a new identity. Aeschylus exploits theatrical principles (and the audience's belief in them) to offer a reassuring conclusion: the logic of the costuming implies that the Erinyes have been changed for good.

The power of costume to impose an identity and to make characters transform or become something new, may also be represented as a dangerous quality. This idea is effectively exploited by Euripides in the *Bacchae*. In this play, the insignia of Dionysus – the fawnskin, the *thyrsus*, and ivy – are represented as capable of transforming those who wear them. This is first made clear in the scene with the two old men, Cadmus and Teiresias, who have both agreed to put on the insignia of the god (lines 174-80), and appear on stage wearing it. They claim to be experiencing the effects of worshipping Dionysus; so, for example, they both feel a sense of rejuvenation (lines 187-90). The implicit logic here is that putting on the insignia has transformed them, so that it offers a neat analogy to theatre costume and its principle of transformation which we have already seen in operation. The old men are transformed by the insignia just as Dicaeopolis is by Telephus' costume. Dionysus' insignia collectively is referred to as *skeue* (see lines 34 and 915), a term which was equally applicable to theatre costume too; this shared term makes the identification of the insignia as analogous to costume all the more obvious. It was, furthermore, entirely appropriate to think of the insignia (which are also in this context, pieces of costume), through this double gaze, since Dionysus is god of theatre and this aspect of the god is implicitly exploited throughout this play (see Foley 1980). From this perspective, the characters within the playworld wear the traditional insignia of maenads (female worshippers of Dionysus) to worship Dionysus, while the actors put on theatre costume also in a context of worship of this god (i.e. the Dionysia festival in celebration of Dionysus). Putting on the insignia has transformational effects in the same way as Telephus' costume had, but this time there is a sense of danger to it. The idea that the pieces of costume, which are also insignia, are somehow dangerous and responsible for the transformation of these men, is reinforced by the way in which Pentheus reacts to it. When he catches sight of the old men dressed up in these insignia, he says (Euripides, *Bacchae* 248-54, tr. Seaford 2001):

> But here is another wonder: I see the diviner in dappled fawnskins, Teiresias,
> and the father of my mother – how laughable! – being a bacchant with a fennel-rod.
> I reject, sir, the sight of your old age without sense. Will you not shake off the ivy?
> Will you not free your hand of the thyrsus, father of my mother?

Pentheus' insistence that Cadmus should take off the insignia can be understood as coming from a conviction that these bits of costume are responsible for the way in which Cadmus is thinking and behaving; he has 'become' a bacchant. Pentheus' response to the costume adds another layer to its symbolism – it now carries a sense of danger. Thus what was initially a rather light-hearted scene becomes much more serious – in part because of this shift in the perception of the costume. Euripides really exploits the potential of tragic costume and the idea that it represents and dictates identity in order to create this sense of danger. These two characters have put on insignia and are now acting in a way that is beyond their control. They are, in this respect, just like the women of Thebes whom, Dionysus tells us at the opening of the play, he has sent mad and forced to wear the trappings of his mysteries (lines 32-4). Dionysus' lines hint at the same connection between behaviour and insignia that we have seen in action in the case of the old men.

In this same scene, the old men will try to persuade Pentheus to join them in worshipping Dionysus and Cadmus will even make a physical attempt to wreathe his grandson's head in ivy (lines 341-2); Pentheus is appalled and tells him to keep his hands off. The violence of Pentheus' reaction against this attempt demonstrates the strength of his belief in the insignia's dangerous power to transform. Eventually, of course, even Pentheus will give way and find himself putting on the costume of a bacchant with dire consequences (for discussion of this see Chapter 5). We are told in the messenger speech (lines 1114-21) that just before his death, Pentheus tries to undo the effect of his costume by removing the sash from his hair in an attempt to get his mother to recognise him, but his action is not enough to reassert his identity – the semiotics of his assumed costume are too powerful. In this play, Euripides takes full advantage of costume's accepted ability to transform and uses this as a way of reading Dionysian insignia, and vice versa the transformational powers of Dionysus and his insignia become a way of understanding the effect of theatre costume. In this respect the *Bacchae*, which beneath its surface is closely engaged in reflecting on theatre, offers a further comment to the discussion about the transformational power of costume which Aristophanes had opened up with the costume-borrowing scene in his *Acharnians* 393-489.

II. Determinism

Not only does a costume have the potential to be closely associated with a certain character identity, but it is also possible for pieces of tragic costume to symbolise or suggest a certain plotline or fate. The two ideas are, in fact, closely connected, since often it is through the association with a character, and what happens to them, that the costume is able to point to a certain plotline. So, for example, this is the case for both of the comic examples of adopting another's stage costume that we have discussed. Dicaeopolis and Dionysus put on the costumes of Telephus and Heracles respectively, in part to be imbued with their character traits, but also implicitly in the hope that things will turn out for them as it did for the character they imitate; for Dicaeopolis this will mean that his speech will turn out well and for Dionysus it means making it down to the underworld and back again. There is a sense in which the fate of a stage character is embedded in the costume along with the words he/she has spoken and his/her character traits. So that, if only Dicaeopolis can get hold of Telephus' costume, he feels sure that things will work out well.

This idea that costume could somehow have an impact on the direction of the play, or from the character's point of view their fate, cannot have been so difficult for a fifth-century audience to accept, since it seems that there was a widespread belief that even in everyday life clothing's symbolism could have an impact on one's destiny. This idea comes up in the fifth-century Hippocratic medical treatise *The Sacred Disease* II.23-4 where the attempts of doctors, characterised as charlatans, to explain and treat diseases are ridiculed. Listed among the sham treatments that these 'quacks' might come up with is advising patients against the wearing of black, since it is the sign of death. For this advice to be taken seriously, the patient must have accepted that clothing had some ability to influence outcomes. Although this advice is clearly meant to seem ridiculous to the reader of the treatise, if it could be suggested at all (either in reality or hypothetically), then it seems that it reflected a widespread superstition held by at least a portion of the society.

Euripides exploits the theatrical potential of this idea that a character's clothing could somehow influence the outcome of events or determine their fate in his tragedy *Heracles*. In this play, Heracles' family have been condemned to death by the tyrant Lycus while Heracles is away. When the hero returns he is appalled to discover their situation and sets out to put things right by killing Lycus. Heracles' recognition of the gravity of the situation comes primarily from the way in which his family is dressed when he arrives – he reacts to it with alarm and it prompts further enquiry. In fact his wife Megara, his two sons and his father are all wearing 'death clothing', that is, the clothing that they would normally be dressed in once dead. Part of the *pathos* here is that on being condemned to death, they had begged to be allowed to dress in this clothing in preparation for death and in the recognition that there would be no one left who could dress their corpses. There is much emphasis put on the clothing: first in Megara's request to be allowed to put it on (329), then in Lycus' granting of permission (333-5), and at the family's return to stage dressed in it, it is commented on by the chorus (442-3) which adds to the visual impact and symbolic force of the moment. When Heracles arrives he is struck by the appearance of his family and comments on it, again refocusing the audience's attention onto the clothing (Euripides, *Heracles* 525-6, tr. Barlow 1996):

> But look, what's this? My children before
> the house, their heads covered in funeral wreaths?

The comment creates tension, since the audience knows exactly why the family is dressed in this way and now they wait for the moment that Heracles will discover the reason and react to it. At the same time, the audience must feel anxiety that the symbolism of the clothing and the fate that it points to, namely death, might win out despite Heracles' arrival. In a sense, the characters may have condemned themselves the moment that they put on the clothing. Meanwhile, Euripides continues to heighten the tension and anxiety by drawing further attention to the clothing. At 548, Heracles asks directly: 'But why do the clothes of the children appear like to those of the dead?' This allows him to discover the full implications of the outfits, and once he realises its symbolism or what it portends, he is keen to mediate it by physically manipulating the costume; he instructs his children to throw these wreaths of death from their hair (562). By asking them to do this, he is trying to nullify the symbolic implications of the wreaths. In this respect his demand is just like Pentheus' to Cadmus (see above). Pentheus wants Cadmus to take off the insignia of Dionysus in order to 'undo' its power. Similarly, Heracles wants the children to remove the wreaths because of the fate they suggest. Heracles tries to control the influence of the costume and therefore change the direction of events by asking the children to remove a part of it. We cannot know whether the children obey and throw off the wreaths or not. The text of the play leaves it open to a modern director's discretion, but even if they engage in this stage action they are still left wearing the death clothing. Even though this 'death clothing' might be open to reinterpretation, since it is in fact simply finery (finely woven and expensive garments, referred to by the Greek term *kosmos*), nevertheless in this play its death symbolism has been so explicitly and emphatically set up that it would take more than the removal of a wreath to alter the costume's meaning. And in the end, the final proof of Heracles' failure to modify the costume sufficiently and to redirect the fate determined by its symbolism is offered in the death of Megara and the children. The symbolism of the costume wins out so that Megara and the children will appear on stage as corpses in this clothing, just as the audience must, on some level, have always suspected, or been afraid, that they would.

The costume may in some way be thought of as responsible for the death of these characters in this play. But there is far more subtlety to the fatal power of this costume than there is in the poisoned robe that kills the princess in Euripides' *Medea* or Heracles in Sophocles' *Women of Trachis*. In the case of the poisoned robes, there is still the possibility of dramatic impact and the creation of tension through the question of whether the recipient will put it on and if they do, whether it will kill them. Yet there is a much greater potential for tension and anxiety where the fatal power of the costume is based on something as slippery as symbolism. There is nothing about the death clothing which is literally fatal: there is no poison in it that will kill the characters. So the playwright may allow the audience to entertain a cruel hope that, even if the characters put it on, it may not end up meaning what it seems to or resulting in what it technically should. The audience is emotionally manipulated as Euripides plays with their hope that the ending portended by the costume could be undone: here is Heracles and he will even try to adjust the costume and remove a bit to 'undo' its power. But his attempt to intervene is, in the end, futile. The audience sit, understanding the deadly force of the costume only too well, but are powerless to stop its effect. Meanwhile the costume's symbolism drives forward the action of the play and leaves the audience with an unpleasant sense of completion, or fulfilment, when finally Megara and the children appear as corpses dressed in it. The dangerous power of costume's symbolism, and its ability to determine outcomes, is clearly demonstrated in this play and is central to its emotional impact on the audience.

The awareness of costume's potential in this respect goes back earlier than Euripides. Aeschylus, too, builds tension by playing on the meaning of costume and, through this, toying with the audience's expectations over the outcome of the action of the play. He uses this technique to great effect in his tragedy the *Suppliants*, a play which we have already looked at in Chapter 3 for the attention that it gives to the process of reading costume. In the play, the daughters of Danaus have come as suppliants to Argos and are asking its king, Pelasgus, for protection from their cousins, the sons of Aegyptus, who intend to marry them. We have already looked at the part of the play where Pelasgus encounters the women for the first time and tries to decode their costumes in order to understand who they are and what they want. At the end of his interview with them, the focus returns again to their costumes but this time it is the women who draw attention to them. This verbal manipulation of the costume completes a frame with the earlier discussion of it at the opening of the scene, and this mirror position perhaps alerts the audience to the fact that this exchange, too, will engage with the language of costume in a serious way. This passage plays on exactly the principle of costume symbolism that Pelasgus had set out in his opening recognition that the full significance of their costume can only be communicated by a 'voice to explain' it (245). In some ways, the women's verbal manipulation of their costumes here can be seen as the fulfilment of Pelasgus' earlier invitation to them to offer an explanation. This invitation had been more dangerous than he realised. Through it Pelasgus had established a model for investing costume with meaning through verbal manipulation, which in this exchange is turned against him (Aeschylus, *Suppliants* 455-67, tr. Sommerstein 2009):

> **Cho.** Listen to the conclusion of my many respectful words.
> **Pel.** I am listening. Speak on; it will not escape me.
> **Cho.** We have girdles and belts to hold our robes together.
> **Pel.** I suppose that is appropriate for women to have.
> **Cho.** Well, these, I tell you, give us a fine method –
> **Pel.** Say what words these are that you are going to utter.
> **Cho.** If you don't make a promise to our band that we can rely on –
> **Pel.** What is your girdle-method meant to achieve?
> **Cho.** To adorn these images with votive tablets of a novel kind.
> **Pel.** These words are a riddle. Speak plainly.
> **Cho.** With all speed – to hang ourselves from these gods.
> **Pel.** I hear words that flay my heart.
> **Cho.** You understand! I have opened your eyes to see more clearly.

As a final means of persuading the king to help them, the women in fact here use a threat made through, and made effective by, their costumes. The exchange centres on the question of what their 'girdles'/belts/sashes symbolise. The king has a simple reading of the 'girdles'; for him they are merely an indication of gender since they are 'appropriate for women'. They pose no threat on this reading. But the chorus push further in hinting at an alternative symbolism, at the same time as framing this other meaning as a threat: 'If you don't make a promise to our band that we can rely on –'. The tension builds, added to by the quick pace of the *stichomythia* (line by line exchange), as the king continues to fail to see their meaning and the audience are left second-guessing what is being hinted at. Finally, in response to the king's demand that they tell him plainly, the women explain that they are threatening to hang themselves using their 'girdles'. The horror of this threat is not only in the prospect of their death but in the pollution (*miasma*) that this would bring to the city, since they specify that they would hang themselves upon the holy shrines. Similarly, the Erinyes in Aeschylus' *Eumenides* try to get their own way by threatening to bring *miasma* on Athens. But here, it is the costume which will play an integral role in bringing that pollution. By the end of the exchange Pelasgus' perception of the 'girdles' has changed: he has gone from seeing them as symbols of womanhood and now sees them as potential weapons which could harm not only the women but his city too. It is by successfully making Pelasgus view the 'girdles' in a new way that the chorus is able to make their threat effective, and this depends on their skill at the verbal manipulation of costume. The series of questions and answers invests the 'girdles' with meaning, and it is their final word on it which fixes the dominant meaning in this cluster of symbolism. This final word and the claim to have made Pelasgus see more clearly leave no room for an alternative symbolism; the women imply that their reading is the correct one. The question which symbolism wins out becomes crucial in light of costume's potential to influence outcomes. This exchange, in fact, offers the audience the prospect of two possible endings. On the traditional reading of the 'girdles', which Pelasgus offers first, they are symbols of womanhood. If the king and the audience continue to think of the 'girdles' through this symbolism, then the women's hint at removing their 'girdles' in order to decorate the images/statues in the shrine, in fact carries a very different meaning from the one which they intend. Since loosening the 'girdle' was primarily associated with the wedding night and was a euphemism for the loss of virginity (see, for example, Homer, *Odyssey* 11.245 and Alcaeus, fr. 42.9-10), the women's words potentially suggest an alternative ending to the audience. At this point, the audience is invited to think about the possibility that the women will not be protected by Argos and will therefore soon end up loosening their 'girdles' after marriage to their cousins. The women, however, suggest a different symbolism which imposes a different outcome: their suicide. What makes the threat so dangerous is that they have supported it by embedding their costume with a symbolism which points to that end. In other words, Aeschylus exploits the audience's acceptance of costume's potential to determine fate in order to make the threat here all the more powerful and properly horrifying both to Pelasgus and the audience. Part of the horror must also be created by an archetypally female piece of clothing being transformed (through symbolism rather than action here) into a potential instrument of death and the power shift this implies; Euripides creates a similar impact with his handling of costume in *Hecuba* (see Marshall 2001a).

While Heracles had been desperate to cancel out a dominant fate-shaping symbolism by physical manipulation of the costume in question, the daughters of Danaus are set on constructing a fate-shaping symbolism for their costume through verbal manipulation. Both operate relying on the same principle and the audience's acceptance of it, but we see each playwright using it in a slightly different way. Arguably there is greater tension in the *Suppliants* passage created through the ambiguity of the symbolism and therefore the uncertainty about what outcome exactly is

73

being threatened. On the other hand, the clarity of the death-clothing symbolism (the fate it points to is never in doubt) gives a greater sense of an almost mechanical inevitability to the ending of the *Heracles*.

Euripides' *Suppliants* offers a final example of this technique and shows another variation of it through the combination of aspects from both the *Heracles* and Aeschylus' *Suppliants*. There is the tension created through a character trying to interpret and understand the symbolism (and therefore fate) being suggested by a costume (like Pelasgus), but there is also an over-riding momentum to the scene, and its inevitable end, to anyone who can understand what the clothing symbolises (as in the *Heracles*). Again, it is the symbolism of death clothing which is at the centre of the scene, but this time its ambiguity is played on. The situation is that the widows of the seven champions, who fought against Thebes, have come to Athens to ask for the city's support in their effort to persuade Thebes to hand back the bodies of these dead champions. Iphis, the father of one of these widows, Evadne, comes looking for her just at the point when she is poised ready to leap onto the pyre where her husband's corpse burns (presumably imagined behind the stage building). The tension of this moment is heightened by the audience's awareness of what her costume symbolises and the fate that it points to, since Evadne has just explained her intention and so reveals the meaning of her finery (*kosmos*). Iphis, however, cannot understand why she is dressed as she is, and by the time its fatal meaning is clarified it is too late. Again, it is through the interrogation of *stichomythia* that the character who is at a loss reaches an understanding of the costume's symbolism. Iphis arrives and asks the chorus if they have seen his daughter, Evadne replies from on top of a rock (presumably the stage building) (Euripides, *Suppliants* 1045-71, tr. Coleridge 1938):

> **Ev.** Why question them?
>   Here I am upon the rock, father, over the pyre of Capaneus,
>   Like some bird hovering lightly, in my wretchedness.
> **Iph.** What wind has blown you here, child? What was your errand?
>   Why did you pass the threshold of my house and seek this land?
> **Ev.** It would only anger you to hear what I intend,
>   and so I do not want you to hear, father.
> **Iph.** What! does your own father not have a right to know?
> **Ev.** You would not judge my purpose wisely.
> **Iph.** Why do you deck yourself in that apparel?
> **Ev.** This robe conveys a strange meaning, father.
> **Iph.** You have no look of mourning for your husband.
> **Ev.** No, the reason why I am decked in this way is new, perhaps.
> **Iph.** Do you then appear before a funeral-pyre?
> **Ev.** Yes, for here it is I come to take the prize of victory.
> **Iph.** What victory do you mean? I want to learn this from you.
> **Ev.** A victory over all women on whom the sun looks down.
> **Iph.** In Athena's handiwork or in prudent counsel?

74

Ev. In courage; for I will lie down and die with my lord.
Iph. What are you saying? What is this foolish riddle you propound?
Ev. To that pyre where dead Capaneus lies, I will leap down.
Iph. My daughter, do not speak thus before the multitude!
Ev. The very thing I wish, that every Argive should learn it.
Iph. No, I will never consent to let you do this deed.
Ev. It is all one; you shall never catch me in your grasp. See!
  I cast myself down, no joy to you, but to myself and to
  my husband blazing on the pyre with me.

Evadne is dressed in finery (*kosmos*). The audience know, after she has shared her intention, that this finery had been put on as death clothing. Some people in the audience would have seen the performance of Euripides' earlier play *Alcestis* in 438 BC, a play in which a young woman, Alcestis, explicitly dresses up in finery (lines 160-1) in preparation for her death. For those who had experienced this previous production, the symbolism of the death clothing and the end that it pointed to, would be all the more real, since they had witnessed it fulfilling its meaning and leading to the expected outcome on stage before. Iphis, however, cannot understand why his daughter has chosen to dress up like this. He makes an explicit comment about how he cannot make sense of it, since it is inappropriate as mourning wear. The appropriate choice of outfit would be in a dark fabric and should be accompanied by a lack of concern for her appearance, but instead he finds her all dressed up. His suggestion of what she should be wearing almost sets up an alternative ending, at least in the imagination of the audience, since had she been in mourning wear it would have pointed to her husband's death but not to her own. But this alternative can only remain illusory, so long as she is standing there visible before the audience and dressed in finery. The only thing that could save her would be the mediation of the meaning of her costume, but since Iphis cannot understand what it points to, he is hardly in a position to construct an alternative symbolism for it. In fact, unlike in *Heracles*, the audience can have little hope of mediation at this point or the undoing of the driving force of the costume to its destined end as death clothing on a corpse. All Iphis' attempts to try to understand the costume only put further emphasis for the audience on its very obvious meaning. Again, the emotional effect on the audience is, in part, based on the sensation of powerlessness on their part (they may understand the costume but they can do nothing to change its meaning). Here, Evadne has all the control, both because she, like the daughters of Danaus, has a much clearer grasp on the game she is playing and on how to manipulate her costume verbally, but also because she has the spatial advantage. She, like Medea at the end of Euripides' play, is shown to have control through the superior height which she has over the man whom she defies.

The dynamic of this passage is, therefore, different from what we have seen in either *Heracles* or Aeschylus' *Suppliants*, since here the audience are certain of the meaning of the costume and experience the *pathos* evoked by watching a father fall short of understanding it and so fail to save his daughter. The outcome is never really in doubt, and the seriousness of the possibility that the finery will lead to death is enhanced for any audience member who had watched the same process of dressing in finery and dying in the *Alcestis*. Here the playwright could take advantage of performance history, and the training that it had given the audience in the language of costume, in order to build up the layers to this moment and add to its dramatic impact. The effect of the death clothing, however, is even more striking in the *Suppliants* through the swiftness and violence with which its symbolism is fulfilled. This also sets this scene in the *Suppliants* apart from the moment in Aeschylus' *Suppliants* which we have discussed, since in Aeschylus' play, even though the establishment of the symbolism is just as intense and emotionally affecting, the potential consequences of the symbolism are never lived out. The 'girdles', once the women have embedded them with their chosen symbolism, hold as much promise of violence as Evadne's finery, but in fact they will remain an unfulfilled threat. The experience of Euripides' *Alcestis*, as well as his *Suppliants*, could (to the audience members who had watched those productions) add further layers to the emotional responses to the death clothing in his *Heracles*. Again Euripides can profit from performance history in order to heighten the effect, since the audience's certainty that putting on this clothing will prove fatal is strengthened by past experience. Euripides plays with the strength of this conviction by giving some hope that there might be a way of escaping the end determined by the costumes. There had been no such hope in *Alcestis* or in *Suppliants* (even if Alcestis is brought back to life she has to die first), but here there is physical intervention by Heracles (where he tells them to take off the wreaths). Even so, the costume's symbolism wins out, but the richness of the emotional journey on the way to that determined end is in part created through the comparisons with past experiences of costume, which at least some of the audience would make. These three plays demonstrate the possibilities and variations that just one principle of the language of costume could open up to the playwrights. It is also clear from these examples that as the years of performance history grew, so too did the range of examples of the language of costume in use, and that this enabled subsequent plays to nuance even further the dramatic effect produced by costume.

III. Emotional manipulation

Costume can be used by characters to try to produce a particular emotional response from other characters. We have already looked at the example of Electra in Euripides' *Electra* who comments on the wretched state of her clothing at line 185. This verbal comment confirms to the audience that her costume should be understood to represent her poor state, but at the same time it functions within the play as a means through which Electra tries to evoke the pity of the choruswomen. The comment activates her costume as an agent of emotional manipulation. The chorus cannot escape from thinking about her wretched state, since she has made her clothing into a visual symbol of it and one which rests right before their eyes throughout the action of the play. At the same time as manipulating the chorus in the play, Electra's words, and the emphasis they place on the symbolism of her costume, also potentially have an emotional impact on the audience.

In other cases, it is the playwright, rather than the character, who tries to manipulate the audience's emotions through his costuming strategy. The difference in these cases is that the character, who wears the costume or comments on it, does not seem to have the same deliberate intention of manipulation. Whereas Electra's comments are self-conscious and deliberately chosen for a particular effect (she is in control of her costume's symbolism and its emotional impact), other characters may comment in a way which, almost inadvertently, activates an emotional response in the audience. One example of this is offered in Euripides' *Hippolytus* when Theseus returns to discover that his wife has committed suicide. In his response to the news he draws attention to the inappropriateness of the garland that he is wearing (Euripides, *Hippolytus* 806-10, tr. Davie 2003):

> **Theseus** Ah, why is my head crowned with this leafy garland
> when the god has repaid my visit with misery? Open up the
> doors that bar the entrance, you servants, undo the fastenings
> that I may see my wife, a sight to wither my eyes, the one
> whose death is death to me.

Theseus has returned from a trip to Delphi as a sacred envoy and is crowned with a garland from there which signifies good fortune. On his arrival, Theseus explicitly mentions where he has been and therefore puts the garland in context for the audience and enables them to interpret its symbolism. This creates an uneasy tension between the happiness communicated by the garland and the evident unhappiness of the chorus which Theseus is quick to comment on. The discomfort of these conflicting signs reaches its height when Theseus discovers what has happened and speaks the lines quoted above. He realises the inappropriateness of what he is wearing and by drawing attention to it with his comment, he heightens the emotional impact of the visual juxtaposition. Before he speaks these words, it is just possible that the garland may have caused only a vague sense of discomfort for some of the audience, but Theseus' words bring the full force of its semiotic potential to evoke emotion into play. His discovery of the news is made more terrible by the clear, and inescapable, sign of good fortune which he wears on his head. The impact of the costume is not only felt at the moment of realisation but throughout his heart-felt and extensive laments which follow, since the audience is confronted with this constant visual reminder of past fortune. The garland is manipulated by Euripides in order to evoke a maximum of *pathos* from the audience for Theseus' reversal of fortune. It acts as a double symbol which at the same time as representing Theseus' past fortune is also capable of pointing to his current wretchedness. In this sense, the garland operates in a similar way to the tattered finery which Xerxes wears in Aeschylus' *Persians* – it reminds the audience both of his previous fortune and his loss of that state (see Chapter 3). While the symbolism of Xerxes' clothing is set up by verbal comments made by his father before he appears on stage (835-6), which are reinforced by his own comments (1030), Theseus is the only one responsible for setting up the symbolism of his garland through his comments. This is not, however, as Electra's comment is, self-conscious or with any deliberate intention, but merely a painful realisation. His comment has a further potential to activate emotional impact on the audience, since it is likely that they too were wearing festival garlands (see the evidence of Athenaeus 11.464 in Csapo and Slater 1994, 4.161, p. 301). When Theseus comments on how inappropriate his garland is in the circumstances, although there is something especially terrible in the fact that he, as the victim of misfortune, is wearing a garland, it is also possible that the audience might feel some discomfort over their own garlands. This seems all the more probable given the nature of the ancient theatre and the curve of the seating which suggests that a spectator would only have to look across the theatre in order to be reminded of the garlands worn by the audience. If Theseus' comment did operate in this way, then it shows costume becoming a means of inviting very close audience identification with the character and his emotional state; all this adds to the emotional impact of this scene.

One of the criticisms of Euripides in Aristophanes' *Frogs* is that he uses costume to make his characters pitiable (lines 1063-4; on this passage see Chapter 5). This criticism implies a simple strategy of dressing characters in wretched clothing in order to create sympathy, but as we have just seen in the example of Theseus in the *Hippolytus*, in fact Euripides is capable of more complex strategies to create *pathos* and heighten the emotional impact of a scenario through costume. In fact, it is not the wretchedness of Theseus' clothing, but the exact opposite, which is used to produce pity in this play. The example shows that it can be more affecting when a piece of clothing which is not inherently pitiable is made so through the dramatic scenario. It is possible that the costume could be used in this way without any direct verbal reference to it. So, for example, in Sophocles' *Antigone* costume might have been used to supplement the emotional impact of her words as she goes to her death. She is condemned to the fate of being walled into a cave and left to starve to death, since she has broken the law by burying her brother. She accepts this fate, but has a long final lament before leaving the stage for the last time. Throughout her lament the imagery of marriage and death is interwoven and increases the *pathos* for this young heroine, who is going to her death at an age when she would normally marry (see Rehm 1994, 59-71). The emotional punch of this moment in the play could be strengthened by costuming, since in ancient Greece young people who died before marriage were customarily dressed in the clothing which they would have worn for their wedding day (see Garland 1985, 25 and 139n.25). This custom was carried over into the tragic world created on the fifth-century stage as the words of Hecuba confirm as she wraps the dead Astyanax in the clothing he should have worn on his wedding day (Euripides, *Trojan Women* 1218-20, tr. Barlow 1986):

> I put upon you the glory of Phrygian robes,
> things that you should have worn at your marriage
> to some pre-eminent Asian princess.

For a woman this clothing was not a wedding dress as such, and certainly it was nothing like the iconic white bridal dresses of our society, but rather fine garments (*kosmos*) that could be worn for this ritual. If Antigone were dressed in these ambiguous garments which could point to her marriage or her death, then the audience would feel all the more keenly the uncomfortable contrast between the happy event for which a living person would normally dress in this clothing and the unhappy reality of the play's action, where Antigone has dressed up in preparation for her imminent death. The costume, like Theseus' wreath, would heighten the sense of reversal and suffering by juxtaposing in the imagination a potential happy scenario for the heroine with a bitter reality. There is also the possibility that the costume plays on the audience's emotions by increasing their sense of foreboding since putting on this clothing in dramatic terms almost seals her fate, as discussed above. The difficulty of the emotional manipulation of costume where it is not directly referred to in the text is that there is no way of proving that Antigone was dressed in the suggested costume. The text, however, makes it seem likely that this costume would have been used to support the effect of the words and certainly the emotional impact of the scene would be heightened by its use. The possibility seems all the more likely when we consider that Euripides exploited the ambiguity of this clothing to dramatic effect in the costuming of heroines in a number of his plays already discussed (above all for Alcestis in *Alcestis* 160-1). It is always worth questioning whether the costume in a tragedy could be used in a scene to support the words or enhance the effect, even where there is not necessarily direct reference to it. The manipulation of costume to impact emotionally on the audience need not always involve a direct reference to the relevant piece of costume, although where it does, such as in the case of Theseus, it allows for an even more powerful and inescapable effect. For further examples of the emotional manipulation of costume, see Taplin (1978, 89-93) on Philoctetes' bow and Wyles (2007, 160-1) on Heracles' weapons.

IV. Ethnicity

Understanding the use of ethnicity in the tragedies depends both on recognising the place of ethnic elements in tragic costume in general and also on appreciating that the meaning of a costume comes from a combination of its material parts and their constructed symbolism. The complexity of approaching ethnic elements and examining how they operate, as well as understanding how a sense of ethnicity is established through costume, shows the sophistication of the language of costume as it emerged.

In the survey of visual evidence for tragic costume in Chapter 1, one of the design features which emerged in the last decades of the fifth century was the fitted wrist-length sleeves. This element of the costume has been explained in terms of practicality: the sleeves are there to disguise the male forearms or for the sake of warmth (see Pickard-Cambridge 1968, 202). If this is the explanation, then this prioritising of practicality came at a price, since the sleeves make a potentially misleading semiotic statement. The problem with the sleeves is that in ancient Greece they were associated with foreign dress. We can see sleeves in use for foreign characters in tragedy from very early on: see the pottery fragments from *c.* 470-450 BC (Fig. 2), and continuing to be presented on stage later in the century (Fig. 6, assuming this vase is a response to a performance, which I think it is). So the sleeves are a puzzle: why incorporate an element that would prove such a semiotic red herring? Some have suggested that the design was borrowed from the garments of the Eleusinian officials (see Bieber 1961, 24-6). Meanwhile a modern scholar has argued that the design was copied from Persian royal dress and was initially introduced by Aeschylus for oriental kings, but was then used for stage tyrants and finally, in response to its popularity, was extended to all tragic characters (see Alföldi 1955). This scheme has since been challenged (see Pickard-Cambridge 1968, 198-202).

Wherever the costume was adopted from, its long fitted sleeves must have carried a foreign association for the audience and this needed to be mediated in some way in order to prevent them from assuming all the characters on stage were non-Greeks! In fact, there is a plausible explanation for how this element of the costume could work through its foreign association to suggest that characters were from the past rather than necessarily foreign (see section V below).

The emergence of long fitted sleeves as part of tragic costume has implications for the semiotics of foreign peoples or barbarians on the stage. If, as I have just suggested, the foreign association of sleeves could be re-read and understood as representative of a past time, rather than indicative of a character's ethnicity, then it deprives the playwright of one of the means of indicating that a character is foreign. If we think back to the pottery fragments showing oriental figures around a pyre (Fig. 2), then

Fig. 19. Theatre-influenced representation of Andromeda, *c.* 400 BC.

the long sleeves would, by this later period, no longer necessarily be capable of suggesting these characters' ethnic origin. To represent a barbarian on stage, once fitted sleeves had become a feature of every costume, it was necessary to use semiotic markers which retained primarily foreign associations. These strong visual markers of foreign peoples include: trousers (*anaxyrides*), pointed headpiece/hat (*tiara*), floppy hat (*kidaris*), and perhaps yellow-dyed slippers (*eumarides*; see Aeschylus, *Persians* 660-1). These pieces of costume remained exclusively representative of foreign peoples and therefore had the semiotic power to suggest the non-Greek origin of a character even where the rest of their costume looked decidedly Greek. So, for example, the Attic kalyx crater which dates to *c.* 400 BC and seems to have been painted in response to Euripides' play *Andromeda* (performed 412 BC), Andromeda's costume almost suggests that she could be a Greek character except for her headwear which gives her away as a non-Greek (Fig. 19).

It is a similar story for the actor to the left on the Pronomos vase (Fig. 9a) who always used to be assumed to be oriental because of the misconstruction of his mask string as a *tiara*. The assumption that his mask had a *tiara* invited the suggestion that he was an oriental king, but without that strong marker, there is nothing in his costume to suggest that he must be foreign. Apart from these specific pieces of costume which could

81

convey to the audience that a character was not Greek, the patterning of the fabric was also indicative. It is not necessarily the case that all elaborately patterned woven fabric suggested foreign origins, since it too could operate, like the sleeves of the costume, to suggest the past (see below). But the sensitivity to the motifs used in the fabric patterning can be seen in action on stage in Euripides' *Hecuba* 733-5 (already briefly discussed in Chapter 3), where Agamemnon spots the corpse of Polydorus and deduces from the cloth that it is wrapped in that the dead man must be Trojan (tr. Collard 1991):

> Ha! What man is this I see dead beside the tents? A Trojan, for the clothes which wrap his body tell me he is no Argive.

Here we have an internal viewer, Agamemnon, commenting on the fabric and directing the audience's reading of it. The success of the comment, and its proposed reading of the shroud, depends on the audience's acceptance of the principle that fabric patterning was ethnically distinctive. By extension of this, it must have been possible to hint at a character's origin through the motifs used in the fabric of his/her costume. The distinctively non-Greek motifs, examples of which we have seen in Chapter 1, include the zig-zag, circles, and dots, whereas Greek motifs seem to have included palmettes, waves, and maeanders.

As well as the physical components and patterning of the material part of the costume, visual and verbal hints might encourage the categorisation of it as non-Greek. This is nicely illustrated by the costumes of the daughters of Danaus in Aeschylus' *Suppliants*. They may have been fairly unexceptional in design, perhaps *chitons* made of simple white linen; their cousins are described as dressed in white (Aeschylus, *Suppliants* 719-20) and Helen, in Euripides' *Helen*, which is set in Egypt, is also costumed in white (lines 1186-7). But visual and verbal hints enable the audience to see this costume as foreign. First, the colouring of the mask and perhaps its features (see lines 278-83) act as a filter on how the audience respond to the costume and probably invites them to read it as representative of foreign dress (the same costume could be interpreted differently in combination with a more Greek-looking mask). Secondly, the chorus' own admittance of who they are in their opening ode invites the audience to see the costume as foreign, and finally Pelasgus' comments about it confirm the reading of it as non-Greek (lines 234-7). In fact, where a costume is fairly neutral, then it can be given a foreign overtone, or layer to its symbolism, either through the verbal or physical manipulation of it.

This possibility may be exploited by a playwright who wishes to give a foreign overtone to a Greek character's costume, and through this attach negative associations to them. During and after the Persian wars, the accusation of medism (collaborating with the Persians) remained legally serious and could have real political implications for the accused, as, for example, Themistocles and Pausanias discovered (see Thucydides 1.126-38). Therefore any foreign overtones to Greek costume would attach negative associations to the character in question. These overtones could be added through verbal comment from another character which could influence the audience's perception of the costume. There is an example of this in Euripides' *Orestes* in which Menelaus makes his return from Troy. At his first entrance, the chorus announce his arrival and comment on his costume, implicitly inviting the audience to see it and interpret it in a certain way (Euripides, *Orestes* 348-51, tr. West 1987):

> But see now, here the king approaches, lord
> Menelaus. And by his elegance he may be
> plainly seen to be of the Tantalids' blood.

The chorus' interpretation sets up the costume and its finery as representative of Menelaus' royalty and the nobility of his bloodline, so that the fineness of his clothing corresponds to his status. But the audience is invited to see this same finery in a different light after Menelaus' father-in-law Tyndareos accuses him of becoming a barbarian (line 485). The comment is not made directly about Menelaus' clothing, but rather is meant to insinuate that he is behaving in an un-Greek way. But in Greek thinking the East was closely associated with luxury and fine clothing so that Menelaus' costume could at this point, in light of the accusation, take on a barbarian appearance. The same technique would not work so effectively, of course, if the visual appearance of the costume were at odds with the reading being imposed on it. But here the accusation, and the interpretation of the costume it invites, is in perfect harmony with the costume and it is this which gives added force to Tyndareus' comment. The new reading of the costume activates the prejudice of the audience and therefore works to win their support for Tyndareus in the debate. The only way for Menelaus to recover from this would be to invite an alternative reading of the luxury of his costume, or even to reassert the original reading of it by the chorus. But since he does nothing to redeem it, the costume remains a symbol of his barbarian tendencies. This use of a foreign overtone applied to a Greek character can be termed 'metaphorical orientalism' (see Sourvinou-Inwood 1997). The great advantage of establishing the overtone, or metaphor, through symbolism rather than a physical piece of costume, such as a *tiara*, is that the playwright does not need to commit to presenting the character in that light throughout the whole play. A different perspective can shift the costume back to suggesting Greek high status, rather than oriental luxury, at a later stage in the play, if it is more dramatically effective to do so. If a strong marker of foreignness is used to suggest metaphorical orientalism, then it would make it more of a challenge to communicate actual ethnic otherness. It would also not leave open the same possibility of shifting perspective of a character between Greek and other, since the semiotic force of the *tiara*, for example, and the actual barbarianism it implies, would be too strong to discount.

There are situations, however, where the shift to an uncompromising view of a character as an actual barbarian might be desirable. Here the physical manipulation of the costume by the addition of a piece of costuming has the potential to shift the audience's reading of it overall. In Euripides' *Medea*, the audience' perception of Medea shifts throughout the play and the level of sympathy depends on how close or distant she seems to them (see Sourvinou-Inwood 1997). Critical to the audience's perception of Medea is the way in which she is costumed. If she is dressed in a way which leaves her fixed as a barbarian in the audience's mind throughout, then it makes a clear difference to their response to what she says and to the play's dynamic overall. So, for example, the impact of her opening on-stage speech to the Corinthian women (lines 214-66), where she will try to gain their sympathy and help, changes depending on whether her costume suggests her foreign origin or her adoption of Greek ways. This speech rests on two major rhetorical strategies (designed to win the chorus' support): appeal to female solidarity and sympathy for her situation as a foreigner. The first of these is forcefully pursued in the section which begins with the striking claim (lines 230-1, tr. Davie 2003): 'Of all creatures that have life and reason we women are the most miserable of specimens!' The second strategy plays out after this bid for solidarity (lines 252-8):

> However, we are not in the same position, you and I. You have your city here and homes where your fathers have lived; you enjoy life's pleasures and the companionship of those you love. But what of me? Abandoned, homeless, I am a cruel husband's plaything, the plunder he brought back from a foreign land, with no mother to turn to, no brother or kinsman to rescue me from this sea of troubles and give me shelter.

After laying the ground with this double-pronged approach, she finally makes her request of the chorus at line 259. The effectiveness of her rhetoric and the overall impact of this speech changes according to how she is presented visually. If Medea is costumed so that she looks like a barbarian, then it weakens her rhetorical strategy of trying to appeal to the female solidarity of the chorus by emphasising their shared lot in life, since there is this visible sign of difference between them. Whereas if she is dressed as a Greek, then her tactic of winning sympathy by emphasising how as a barbarian it is particularly difficult for her, loses much of its force. Equally the shock of her claims in this speech (including the famous comment about childbirth, lines 250-1), will be mediated or exaggerated depending on how she is costumed (if she makes the claim dressed as a barbarian then the audience could reassure themselves that no Greek woman thought like that). Medea could have been costumed in either Greek or barbarian costume, and while we cannot know which it was, it is important to realise that the choice would have had an impact on the audience's response to the play. Sourvinou-Inwood makes the very attractive suggestion that Medea could have been dressed in Greek dress until the murder of children and then oriental dress for final scene (see Sourvinou-Inwood 1997, 289). If this were the case, then the costume change could be very simple, since even the addition of a *tiara* could be enough to tip the perception of the costume from Greek to barbarian, as the example of the Andromeda vase from 400 BC (Fig. 19) demonstrates. Furthermore, this physical manipulation of the costume by the addition of a *tiara* would be reinforced by Jason's reflection that no Greek woman would have dared to do what she had done (lines 1339-40), since this comment categorises her firmly as non-Greek at this point and invites the audience to read the costume as representative of this. Alternatively, if Medea is still in Greek-style costume at this point, then the dramatic impact could be equally effective (implying the dangers of barbarians and the female capacity for disguise). Whichever way Euripides chose to costume Medea, the words of his play are designed, with all the references to her origin, to play against it; either there is a tension between the words and the costume (if it is Greek) or the words emphasise the costume making it a constant visual reminder of her origins, creating a different kind of tension.

The use of ethnicity in costume and its manipulation to create dramatic effect in the tragedies shows the language of costume operating at a sophisticated level. Here much of the effect is on the level of the symbolic, taking advantage of the idea of metaphorical orientalism. One Greek character can easily prejudice opinion against another merely by projecting a foreign reading of his costume through a verbal comment. Games with ethnicity in costume and the emotional manipulation made possible through it are clearly being played elsewhere in the *Orestes* too, where descriptions of footwear serve to imply judgements of characters. We are told in the messenger speech of the Phrygian slave (lines 1369-72 and 1467-70) that he is wearing Persian slippers (*eumarides*), while Helen is in golden sandals (literally golden-sandaled), and Orestes is in strong Mycenaean boots. The Persian slippers and golden sandals (implying luxury) carry foreign associations, whereas Orestes' boots are safely Greek. The implication is that the audience is swayed to feel more sympathy for Orestes at this point through this verbal comment on the costume. Thus ethnicity in costume can be used, as it is one way or another in Medea's speech to the Corinthian women, to elicit an emotional response from the audience and enhance the dramatic impact of a play.

V. Historical dimension

Greek tragedy emerges as a theatrical genre in which the play setting is always in the mythical past. The obvious exceptions to this that we know of, Phrynichus' *Sack of Miletus* (see Herodotus, *Histories* 6.21) and Aeschylus' *Persians*, only serve to highlight the conventional past setting. Costume, as in modern productions, could provide an easy means to create the sense of a past age in the playworld being presented to the audience. One of the ways in which tragic costume was able to do this was by the use of the long-fitted sleeves which are shown used for all characters in the visual evidence from about 430 BC onwards (see Chapter 1). The foreign association of these sleeves could in fact be used to evoke the sense of a past age. This is argued persuasively by Luigi Battezzatto who considers the sleeves in light of the Greek approach to foreign customs as representative of their own past (see Battezzatto 2000). The argument is based on the recognition that the Greeks could think of the past as a foreign country. The conceptual model for this thinking is set out by the fifth-century Greek historian Thucydides at the opening of his *History of the Peloponnesian War* (1.6, tr. Warner 1972 with my emphasis):

> The Athenians were the first to give up the habit of carrying weapons and to adopt a way of living that was more relaxed and more luxurious. In fact the elder men of the rich families who had these luxurious tastes only recently gave up wearing linen undergarments and tying their hair behind their head in a knot fastened with a clasp of golden grasshoppers: the same fashion spread to their kinsmen in Ionia, and lasted there among the old men for some time. It was the Spartans who first began to dress simply and in accordance with our modern taste, with the rich leading a life that was as much as possible like the life of the ordinary people. They, too, were the first to play games naked, to take off their clothes openly, and to rub themselves down with olive oil after their exercise. In ancient times even at the Olympic Games the athletes used to wear covering for their loins, and indeed this practice was still in existence not very many years ago. Even today many foreigners, especially in Asia, wear their loincloths for boxing matches and wrestling bouts. *Indeed, one could point to a number of other instances where the manners of the ancient Hellenic world are very similar to the manners of foreigners today.*

In this passage Thucydides reveals a perspective which sees foreign ways as representative of past Greek ways. The underlying idea is that the Greeks are further ahead in their journey of progress and the foreigners, lagging behind, can therefore offer a window onto the Greek past. This provides an approach to understanding the fitted sleeves which came to be a part of tragic costume. If the sleeves suggest a foreign country, then they may at the same time represent the Greek past. The same argument can be applied to the luxury shown in tragic costume which is prominent in the visual evidence at the same time as the sleeves. Thucydides explicitly states that luxury is a thing of the past for the Greeks. It is also, unsurprising, associated with foreign peoples and especially Asiatic wealth. This leaves the possibility open for luxurious fabric to suggest either status in the past Greek world or foreign associations. The costume may shift between these alternative readings even within the same play. We have already seen, for example, the way in which Menelaus' finery could be viewed both as the natural clothing, given the period, of someone of his status (Euripides, *Orestes* 348-51) and yet also as a sign of foreign influence (line 485). The fitted sleeves and the luxury that emerged as a part of tragic costume may be explained therefore as ways through which the past world of the play setting could be evoked. The exploitation of this conceptual model (the past is a foreign country) to achieve this leaves open the possibility of switching between the past and the present in the same costumes. Unlike costumes in a period drama which commit the action to a given age, the Greek way of evoking the past had this ambiguity to it; this makes the task of analysing the costume more complex but also means that a wider range of effects and symbolism is possible for the ancient playwrights (as we have just seen in the case of Menelaus).

Other pieces of costume, integrated among the past-evoking ones, could invite the audience to think of the action in terms of the present even more directly. We know of at least one example of the use of 'anachronistic' costume on the tragic stage. The costume for Heracles which is shown on the Pronomos vase (Fig 9b), incorporates a bronze muscle-cuirass (Fig. 10). This type of armour was developed in the second half of the fifth century and therefore is technically an anachronistic imposter into the mythical world. Its inclusion in the costuming, however, is evidently not the equivalent mistake to an actor wearing a watch in an epic movie. Instead, costume is being used to create a link with the past and make it meaningful for the present. So, again, this points to a more complex, or sophisticated, approach to the use of costuming in these dramas set in the past. The costume is chosen to enable the audience to watch the action through a double perspective of past and present. The breastplate worn by Heracles could invite the audience to think of this mythical hero in terms of the citizens who had been out fighting in wars for Athens. The identification, which the audience might in any case make between Heracles and themselves, is reinforced through this piece of costume and continually reasserted on the subliminal level. It invites a two-way thought process: of the past in terms of the present and the present in terms of the past. The long sleeves of Heracles' *chiton*, and the past world that these simultaneously suggest, save the analogy from being too obvious, this is not a 'modern day' Heracles retrojected into the mythical past but rather a figure who can be thought of as both past and present. Even if we do not have any other visual evidence for an equivalent appropriation of contemporary dress into tragic costume, we find another example of it implied by the text for Aeschylus' *Eumenides* (see above) and it seems likely that playwrights must have exploited this possibility where it presented itself as dramatically effective.

There is another type of past which could be exploited in order to create meaning through costume and to maximise its dramatic impact: the theatrical past. Every year new productions added fresh material to tragedy's performance history and provided a range of experiences and memories, embedded in the costume, which could be exploited by playwrights in subsequent productions. Individual pieces of costume accumulated layers of meaning during their stage life which could be activated or silenced when they were used in a production (see Sofer 2003). Performance history in relation to costume could be traced by following a particular piece of costume's story or by looking at the way in which an individual character had been costumed over time. The two stories necessarily often overlap, especially where an item becomes associated with a particular character (as we have seen in the case of Heracles and his lion skin). Both ways of looking at costume's performance history could be exploited by the tragedians in their use of costume. So, for example, we have a hint of this idea in Euripides' *Electra* 184-9, where Electra complains that she has nothing decent to wear in order to attend the festival. This comment may gain some of its effectiveness from the fact that Electra had never been represented on the tragic stage in a state of good fortune and therefore she has nothing in the metaphorical wardrobe of her performance history that she could wear.

Again in a comment by Electra, but this time in Sophocles' *Electra*, we get a glimpse of how costume's performance history might have been exploited in tragedy. Electra complains of how difficult it is for her to see Aegisthus sitting on her father's throne and wearing his clothing (lines 267-9). The point is that Aegisthus had plotted together with Clytemnestra and killed Agamemnon, Electra's father, on his return from Troy and ruled in his place since. These events are understood to have taken place before the action of Sophocles' play but in fact, this earlier part of the story had already been dramatised by Aeschylus in his *Agamemnon*. So this leaves open the possibility that Sophocles may have literally represented what Electra complains of: he could have presented Aegisthus in a costume which recalled, in the memory of the audience, the costume of Agamemnon in Aeschylus' play. If he chose to do this, then he would be exploiting the performance history of that particular costume in order to make a statement about Aegisthus: he has usurped Agamemnon's throne and stolen his identity. The choice to present Aegisthus as a kind of double to Agamemnon would also allow Sophocles to underline the cyclical nature of revenge killing – since Aegisthus' murder would be in some sense the re-enactment of the killing of Agamemnon; the same figure created through costume would be extinguished in this act. Finally, this piece of 'ghosting' (see Chapter 3) through costume would also be a possible means for Sophocles to acknowledge that Aeschylus had gone before him in the treatment of this story in tragedy. The 'recycling' of Agamemnon's costume could offer a symbolic comment on Sophocles' reworking of the dramatic treatment and tragic material (for 'recycling', see Carlson 1994a, 1994b). In this sense the visual echo of the costume and the inter-performative allusion it evokes, would be operating much as an intertext designed to acknowledge debt to an earlier work. A related case of haunting and exploitation of theatrical past is the use and rehandling of the death cloth (used to murder Agamemnon) by the three tragedians in their dramatic representations of this same story; this example has been discussed by Anne-Sophie Noel (Grenoble) in an as yet unpublished piece of research. Finally, the axe used in the killing of Agamemnonm – if not in the original production of the *Oresteia* in 458 BC, then perhaps in a re-performance of it – evidently became an established part of the performance tradition and came to 'haunt' the subsequent dramatic reworkings of the myth on the fifth-century stage (see Marshall 2001b).

It is also possible that playwrights could exploit their own past use of costume in order to create meaning or as a shorthand means of communicating what a piece of costume was intended to symbolise. We have seen how Euripides could profit from his past usage of death clothing in the *Alcestis*, so that Evadne's use of it in the *Suppliants* could be all the more effective. It is not only the clothing of costume that could be 'recycled' but also the mask. So, for example, where two plays involved the same character, then the use of the same mask could offer a sense of continuity even when the two plays were performed years apart from one another. It need not have been literally the same mask, since in fact there is evidence to suggest that masks were dedicated to Dionysus after performance (see Green 1982). It is possible, however, that, as with the use of Agamemnon's costume for Aegisthus, the costume could be new but designed to look like the earlier one and by activating the audience's performance memory, allow them to make the connection. This could be used in the same way as the literary figure of the contrast simile might be, in order to point to a difference between the two plays and handling of the characters in them. Euripides may have exploited this possibility in his *Helen* which showed Helen in a radically different situation from the conventional one which put her in Troy during the years of the Trojan war (suggested by Ley 1991, 19). Euripides had represented Helen on stage in the conventional setting of Troy in his *Trojan Women* in 415 BC, but then would show her in Egypt in his *Helen* in 412 BC. If the same, or a similar mask, were used for her in both performances, then it would be a means of drawing attention to the completely different treatment of this same character; so the visual echo could evoke a sense of continuity which was totally contradicted by the setting. At the same time, the use of the same mask would be a means of giving symbolic expression to the fact that it was the same playwright who was creating these very different plays; so here the costume ghosting could be used to an authorial self-reflexive end.

Finally, the ghosting of costume and the inter-performative allusion to a previous production did not have to be produced solely through a visual similarity or echo in the costume design but might be suggested through the way in which a costume was handled. The physical manipulation and rearrangement of a costume could call to mind an earlier production and could enhance the meaning of the play being performed. A verbal allusion or clue might add a further hint to direct the audience's mind back to the previous production or to trigger their memory of it. There is a good example of this kind of ghosting in Euripides' *Heracles* where, after recovering from a fit of madness, Heracles discovers that he has killed his wife and children. His instinctive reaction is to cover himself over with his cloak in shame and to hide himself from the world which he can no longer face (line 1159). The stage action could easily call to mind a moment from Aeschylean drama which had evidently become iconic in the society's performance memory; Aeschylus had presented Niobe on stage all wrapped up in a cloak and saying nothing. We know about this piece of staging from Aristophanes' *Frogs* 911-13 where the character Euripides mocks Aeschylus for it; this makes it clear that this handling of costume in Aeschylus' play had become an iconic moment in the cultural memory (the joke depends on the audience remembering or being familiar with this scene in the earlier production). The point of this inter-performative allusion in the *Heracles* is to add to the poignancy of Heracles' situation by calling to mind another tragic figure who had suffered the death of her children through the interference of the gods. Niobe is the mythic figure *par excellence* through which to think about, and negotiate, extreme grief (see for example Homer, *Iliad* 24.599-617). So the reference to Niobe, made by Euripides through the echo in the manipulation of the costume, deepens the audience's understanding of Heracles' emotional state at this point. It also increases the tension over Heracles' future, since Niobe's traditional end in myth was to turn into a weeping rock and go on mourning forever. The audience already has the connection to Niobe put in mind through Heracles' manipulation of his costume, and it only takes Heracles' wish that he would turn into a rock (line 1397) to direct their attention to this aspect of her myth and the risk of this end for Heracles too. The fear of this is heightened through the audience's conviction that costume was able to determine a given fate (see above). So this echo in the costuming allows Euripides to evoke all the tension and emotion that Aeschylus had built up in his treatment of Niobe and to import it into his own play at a stroke. At the same time, he can also play on the audience's anxiety over how Heracles will resolve his situation (or whether he will simply stay in a liminal state). The brilliant advantage of this kind of allusion created by the physical manipulation of the costume, as opposed to the costume design, is that the allusion could be evoked at a precise moment and the entire performance did not need to be haunted by a previous production or stage presentation of a character. On the other hand, some productions might benefit from the more permanent ghosting through a visual hint in the costume design which constantly confronted the audience with the connection to a past moment on stage.

An appreciation of the theatrical past is essential to understanding the use of costume in any of the Greek tragedies, since the language of costume was an organic thing developing over the fifth century and growing with each performance. The possibilities open to the playwrights and the meanings which could be created depended on that performance history. From this perspective, the chronology of the plays becomes hugely important, if we are to recognise when a playwright might be exploiting an earlier use of costume. It is also a question of trying to reconstruct the visual landscape of the audience's performance memory in order to be able to identify the impact of costume ghosting and the meaning it creates.

VI. Fabrication

The playwright may also exploit the audience's awareness of the mode of production of the costume in order to create another nuance or layer to its meaning. One example of this is offered by Hermione's comments on her costume in Euripides' *Andromache* 147-8, which we discussed briefly in Chapter 2. Hermione's first words in the play are the boasts she makes here, about her fine clothing and her claim that it symbolises her high status which gives her the right to say what she pleases. The dramatic purpose of the emphasis on her fine clothing extends beyond her stated reason for mentioning it; her words activate the costume's meaning as symbols of her high status, but at the same time and at a different level her costume creates *pathos* by the visual contrast it offers with Andromache's poor state. The two women's difference in fortune is clearly expressed by their two costumes and this visually confronts the audience throughout the scene, exerting an influence on how they respond to the words spoken by each character. Hermione's attitude towards her costume makes her characterisation very clear at this first entry and show her to be spoilt, proud, and self-satisfied.

So Hermione's costume and her words about it already function to show her status, to heighten the *pathos* for Andromache, and to demonstrate her character, but there is also possibly another effect which though not dramatically significant, reveals something about Euripides' artistry as a playwright. There is a poetic satisfaction, and perhaps a wry smile, in these lines for those in the audience who gave a thought to the fabrication of this type of fine clothing at this point. The connection could readily be made through the focus on this character's name, Hermione (since it is her first entry and therefore her identity is inevitably a focus point) together with her reference to her fine clothing. This juxtaposition could quite naturally bring to mind the place Hermione which was in fact a site for the production of luxury fabrics (see Reinhold 1970, 22). The connection makes the characterisation of Hermione and the comments that she makes all the more appropriate – of course a character called Hermione would be concerned with luxury fabrics! A similar kind of word play around character names is found elsewhere in Euripidean tragedy, for example there is a pun around the name Pentheus in the *Bacchae* 367. But what is so striking here is that the game is implicit and depends on the audience thinking about the world outside the theatre. Here the costume and the comments on it invite the audience to step away, for a brief moment, from the action in order to enjoy the playwright's wit (on Euripides' sophisticated humour see Winnington-Ingram 1969). This example demonstrates how the theatrical experience could be altered, and ultimately enhanced, by bringing thoughts of the costume's fabrication into the audience perspective. The connection which Hermione's comment invites may not have a major impact on the dramatic meaning at this point, but it nevertheless contributes to the complex texture of the tragic experience, adding a wry smile in amongst the grimness of the suffering portrayed.

The second example of this technique shows it being used in a context where it has much greater significance to the dramatic impact of the scene. The famous moment in Aeschylus' *Agamemnon* 931-72, where Agamemnon is persuaded to tread on the sea-purple cloth which has been spread out on the ground before him, gains a greater impact and even another layer of meaning if the audience reflects on how the cloth used in this scene was made. The text makes it very clear that the cloth is meant to be understood within the playworld to be sea-purple, meaning that it is very costly since it has been dyed using the juice of *murex* molluscs. Clytaemnestra's argument in favour of spoiling the cloth puts emphasis on the dyeing process (lines 958-60, tr. Lloyd-Jones 1982):

> There is a sea – and who shall dry it up? –
> that breeds a gush of much purple, precious as silver,
> ever renewed, for the dyeing of garments.

The dramatic effect depends on the awareness that in this act Agamemnon is spoiling wealth, by ruining something which is costly to make and expensive to buy; the tension over whether Agamemnon will do it or not is heightened greatly if the audience thinks that it is a real sea-purple cloth used in the scene. In theatre, of course, it is perfectly possible to use a cheap imitation to represent the item in question on stage (so for example, glass for diamond). But in the context of the Dionysia and Athenian interest in displaying wealth there, it seems likely that a real sea-purple cloth would have been used (on the lavish expenditure at this festival see Wilson 2000, 94). The use of a real cloth changes the nature of this theatrical moment and dramatic action; the difference is comparable to someone burning what are known to be real bank notes on stage, as opposed to what is recognised to be 'Monopoly' money. The audience would be able to recognise if it were a real sea-purple cloth from its unique shimmering lustre (see Pliny, *Natural History* 9.60-2). Clytaemnestra's words therefore draw attention to the type of cloth and its value not only within the playworld, but also in real life, and direct the audience's focus on this fact precisely at the moment when Agamemnon is in the act of treading on the cloth.

4. Costume in Action

The sight of Agamemnon trampling on what was known to be real sea-purple cloth and actually spoiling wealth on stage would have created a much greater impact, since it would fuse the actual and the representative – the action is happening in reality as well as in the created world of the play; as Agamemnon ruins the cloth, so does the Athenian actor. Through this moment, Athens as a city participates in a public act of spoiling wealth which suddenly makes Agamemnon's fate after this action all the more crucial, since it now implies something for, or about, Athens. The tragic action on stage becomes, for a moment, of direct and inescapable relevance to the audience and perhaps poses a challenge to Athens. Alternatively, it is possible that some members of the audience could view the act out of context and see it as a simple public display of conspicuous consumption showing the greatness of Athens (though I find this kind of disassociated viewing unlikely). In terms of the drama, the identity between the imitated action and reality (i.e. the actor is pretending to trample wealth at the same time as actually doing it), has the effect of making the tension and impact of the stage action all the greater.

The power of this moment depends on Aeschylus exploiting the audience's awareness of how the cloth used in the production has been made. Again, as in the case of Hermione, the technique requires the audience to step back from the action and think of the real world outside the frame of the play. But unlike the case of Hermione, the effect of this stepping back in the *Agamemnon* in fact brings the action closer to the audience and contributes to the dramatic impact created through the cloth and Agamemnon's act of trampling on it. Aeschylus profits from the performance context of his play and especially the desirability of big budget productions at the Dionysia. It is perhaps extraordinary from a modern perspective that when it was probably possible to produce a cheaper imitation of this purple cloth (which would do the job of 'standing' for a sea-purple cloth in performance), it remains more likely that a real sea-purple cloth was used (on imitation purples see Reinhold 1970, 53). But the gain, in terms of the dramatic impact of the moment, is huge. In subsequent productions, of course, imitation purple may have been used and it is even possible that such a measure was employed later in the fifth century as the wealth of Athens dwindled through years of war (revivals of Aeschylus' tragedies were put on in Athens after his death: see *Life of Aeschylus* 1, Aristophanes, *Acharnians* 10-12 and *Frogs* 868-9). In this case, where imitation purple was used, the dramatic moment would lose some of its power, since it remains safely in the realm of representation and restricted to the playworld. But in Roman performances at least, there was an equivalent motivation to spend lavishly on the tragic productions. We know from Horace's complaints about the audience being too easily impressed simply by the Tarentine purple of the tragic actor's costume (Horace, *Epistles* 2.1.182-207) that costly purple could be used in performances. Furthermore, Cicero's account of a production of *Clytaemnestra* (a

Roman tragedy) at the opening of Pompey's theatre in 55 BC suggests that no expense was spared, since he writes that it included 600 mules! (Cicero, *Letters to Friends* 7.1). So the potential to recreate the effect and impact of an actual spoiling of wealth on stage remained, or perhaps re-emerged, in the Roman period. The idea of the possibilities and limitations of costume in later productions of tragedy is discussed further in Chapter 6.

In *Frogs* 1058-68, Aristophanes sets out two models for how a tragedian could use costume in his plays: it is either a means of communicating character status or of evoking emotion. This passage is discussed in more detail in the next chapter, but for now it offers the opportunity to recognise just how sophisticated the actual use of costume in fifth-century tragedy was by comparison. Not only do these two models miss the idea that a costume could have multiple functions at the same time (and therefore could communicate both character status and evoke emotion), but they also overlook the possibilities offered by shifting perspectives which could change the predominant meaning of a costume at any moment in the play. The establishment, or reconfiguration, of a costume's symbolism could be created by its physical or verbal manipulation and could result in a reassessment of the character's identity (or ethnic association), a sealing of fate or its aversion, a painful evoking of emotion, and the zooming of the action backwards in theatre history or forwards to the Athenian present. Looking at the language of costume in action in the plays shows the impressive potential of this semiotic system and the skill with which the playwrights exploited it.

There are two quite unique features to the fifth-century performance context which enable some of the most dramatically effective usages of costume that we have looked at: the use of the mask and the closed-system of the festival. The first allows the absolute identity of costume with character and the second ensures a strong performance memory in the audience; together these create a rare opportunity for playing with the possibilities of inter-performative allusion and ghosting. The unusual set of circumstances in which the language of costume was developed and expanded make the fifth century a particularly interesting potential case-study of semiotics. Understanding how costume in Greek tragedy operates, therefore, not only enhances our appreciation of these plays but also offers interesting food for thought in the history of theatre.

Costume and Theatrical Discourse

In Chapters 3 and 4, the focus was on how the language costume operated and was used to create meaning within the plays. In this chapter, we will be considering costume from a different angle. Rather than looking at how costume's manipulation created meaning in the immediate context of the play and its action, we will think about how costuming strategies could contribute to an on-going commentary on another level. Throughout the fifth century, at the same time as there being a line of development for the language of costume through its various applications in different productions, it is also possible to trace the shape of a discussion within the plays about theatre as an artform. No critical discourse or treatise about theatre and how it worked survives from fifth-century Athens, but the question was nevertheless being engaged with in the plays themselves. The handling of costume in both tragedy and comedy often contributes implicitly to this discussion or theatrical discourse. Costume, in fact, provides an easy means through which to make a comment on theatre, since it is so fundamental to its creation; thinking about the process of dressing up in costume necessarily also invites, on some level, reflection on how theatre works or is created. Thus many of the passages which we have already looked at when trying to establish how the language of costume operated, and was understood to work, are also important for the commentary they provide on theatre in general. We will look again at these passages, as well as others, in order to trace the outline of this discourse as it developed across the century. This outline will not, of course, include every single part of the discourse, since I do not discuss every surviving play to comment in this way, and many plays, which may too have contributed comments of this nature, are now lost or fragmentary. But the outline should, nevertheless, give an idea of how costume could be used to make comments on this broader level. It should also offer insight into the general understanding of how theatre worked and notions of how it should be done.

If we start with the earliest passage that we looked at, then we can see a beginning to this theatrical discourse through costume, in Aeschylus' production of his *Suppliants* in 463 BC. In this play, as we saw in Chapter 3, there is an internalised reflection of the audience's semiotic process when reading theatre costume. On some level, at this moment in his play Aeschylus invites the audience to step back from the immediate action and to think about how theatre works. This part of the scene makes the audience aware of what it is that they do when they go to watch a piece of

theatre. They, like Pelasgus, try to interpret and decode the visual information presented before them in the costumes. This semiotic process,
which they become self-conscious about, does not pertain to costumes
exclusively; it is just as relevant and applicable to the entire theatrical
event and the spectacle of what is put on stage. So that, although the scene
is directly concerned with inviting the audience to think about costume
and their process of interpreting it, they may also at the same time
consider how inherent that semiotic process of decoding is to theatre in
general and their understanding of what the playwright shows them.
Importantly, while there is a hint of the metatheatrical here, since Pelasgus' comments and his place as an internal spectator almost offer the
audience the view of a play within a play (or at the very least set them at
a double remove from the action), this is not explicit. Tragedy as a general
rule, unlike comedy, does not openly comment on theatre or deconstruct it
on stage in front of the audience. Yet clearly the commentary on costume
offered here comes close to a type of metatheatre, since it makes a
contribution to a theatrical discourse. The discussion of the artform is in
the subtext and the technique of commenting through the handling of
costume helps to keep it there. But a part of what we will see in the
continuation of this embedded discourse is that the response to it in
comedy brings the subtext closer to the surface in tragedy.

The next point in the line comes in 438 BC with the production of
Euripides' *Telephus* which now survives only in fragments, but from the
engagement with this tragedy in Aristophanes' *Acharnians* it becomes
apparent that Euripides was on some level concerned with thinking about
theatre in this play. In Euripides' play the hero Telephus took on a
disguise as a beggar and so was presented in a ragged costume. The use of
disguise in the play offered a ready way for thinking about theatre, since
disguise offers an easy analogy to theatre costume; both involve dressing
up in order to assume a different identity (see Muecke 1982a). We have
further confirmation that Euripides took advantage of this analogy and
invited the audience to think about the theatrical process, from two of
Telephus' lines which are quoted by Dicaeopolis in Aristophanes' *Acharnians* 440-1 (see Chapter 3 and *TGrF*, fr. 698 with Collard et al. 1997, 28).
Even if the quotation is not exact, the gist of it is enough to suggest an
engagement with the question of how theatre works; in effect, Telephus
says that he has to seem to be a beggar and conceal his real identity. This
notion is applicable to theatre in general and so it seems that this now
fragmentary tragedy was at least in part concerned with exploring the
nature of theatre. This shows once more that it is on the level of costuming
that playwrights could quite naturally (without breaking the conjured
presence of the playworld) contribute to theatrical discourse; so that, while
the audience might read costume thinking about its implications for the
play, they were also prepared for it to be operating at this other level too.

Aristophanes' *Acharnians* in 425 BC picks up the thread of the discourse which Euripides had engaged with in his *Telephus*. The commentary on theatre which most likely operated on the level of subtext in the *Telephus*, Aristophanes brings to the surface in his *Acharnians* in the scene we have already looked at where Dicaeopolis goes to Euripides' house to borrow a costume (lines 393-489). The disguise of rags which in the *Telephus* seems to have represented theatre costume on an implicit level, in *Acharnians* becomes theatre costume on an explicit level. This is a means for Aristophanes to signal that he is going to engage in theatrical comment more directly and, at the same time, he may wish to make the assertion that comedy was better suited to the task. In comedy, as is shown by the example of the direct comment on the management of the stage crane in Aristophanes' *Peace* 174, it was possible to break the illusion and expose the mechanics of theatre and this perhaps made it the better genre for engaging in theatrical discourse. But in fact, as we have seen, tragedy could contribute to it too, just at a different level, and it seems that one of the advantages of having these two types of theatre running along side by side annually was the possibility for this dialogue about theatre to be bounced back and forth between them, since the two means of commenting (one implicit, the other explicit) in fact complement one another. Comedy could benefit from the shorthand that tragedy's treatment of costume offered (so that Telephus' rags already hint at theatrical comment – it is a part of what they represent after the performance). Equally, as we will see, tragedy could respond to comments made in comedy and profit from that genre making the questions being engaged in more explicit.

The costume-borrowing scene in the *Acharnians* 393-489, as we have already established in Chapter 3, explores the question of how theatre costume works to create a stage character. But this is not all that Aristophanes is interested in discussing through the scene. He is also commenting on Euripides' way of doing tragedy or more generally of creating theatre. The criticism of Euripides as too gimmicky or a fan of special effects is implicit in the way in which he appears – he cannot come to the door and so is made to appear by using the *ekkyklema* (roll-out platform) (Aristophanes, *Acharnians* 407-8). A related criticism is made about his use of costume and by extension his dramaturgy (way of doing theatre). When Dicaeopolis comes and asks to borrow some rags, he is in fact offered the rags of six other Euripidean characters before finally acquiring Telephus', which were the ones he wanted. This is partly for the sake of comic effect, but there is also a more serious point being made about Euripidean drama. The implication is that Euripides has overdone the tragic-character-in-rags device, so that it is no longer dramatically effective or, even worse, it has become potentially ridiculous (see Muecke 1982a, 21).

The criticism of Euripides' approach to costuming, and therefore theatre, is pushed further at the close of the scene. Dicaeopolis asks to borrow more and more props, until Euripides complains that he is being robbed of all his tragedies by this (lines 464 and 470). So Aristophanes implies that Euripides' plays and tragic art are entirely dependent on costume (including props). The same criticism will be reiterated by him through the character Aeschylus in his *Frogs* in 405 BC, where the implications of this dramaturgical approach will be explored a bit more fully (see below). Here Aristophanes seems to be suggesting that Euripides is too dependent on visual effects in his drama. Part of how he makes this point is to present Euripides surrounded by costumes which represent his plays, either symbolically or literally (see Macleod 1974). His plays are nothing more than the costumes that make them up and even these are used over and over again. The idea of repetition and reuse is suggested not only through the elaborate catalogue of all the rags that Dicaeopolis could borrow, but also by the representation of Euripides in the act of composition surrounded by the costumes of characters from his old plays. The implicit point is that Euripides takes inspiration for his new works from the costumes used in the old ones. While costume is fundamental to creating theatre, a dramaturgy based principally on this was clearly considered inadequate. It seems possible that Aristophanes criticises this aspect of Euripidean drama partly from the motivation of protecting his own territory – perhaps in his view it should be comedy which has the monopoly on dramatic impact through visual effect. Wherever his motivation for the criticism came from, the scene demonstrates beautifully how costume could be used to talk about theatre and dramaturgy more generally.

Aristophanes returns to the question of costume, composition, and the operation of theatre in his *Women at the Thesmophoria*, produced in 411 BC. We have already looked at the scene where Inlaw borrows a female disguise from the effeminately presented tragedian Agathon (lines 39-279). Our focus was on what Inlaw's reaction to Agathon could reveal about the semiotic process of reading tragic costume. The treatment of the figure of Agathon in this scene certainly has much to say about theatre, the process of becoming a character, and the seductive characterisation of tragedy, on which see Duncan (2006). Interesting also is the point at which Inlaw gets dressed up as a woman. This part of the scene corresponds to the stage presentation of Dicaeopolis getting dressed up as Telephus. Although Inlaw is not technically putting on a theatre costume (it is understood to be from Agathon's own wardrobe rather than from one of his past plays), by analogy and viewed with the scene in the *Acharnians* in mind, it becomes clear that his action is intended as a comment on the process of putting on theatre costume. In this sense the ghosting by the *Acharnians*, created by the echo in scenario, is partly responsible for constructing the meaning here. So what does the sequence of Inlaw's dressing add to the discourse on theatre? Or in other words, what statement does Aristophanes make through it? The presentation of the process of a man dressing as a woman is undeniably funny. Aristophanes makes it deliberately so by playing up Inlaw's reluctance and his inadequacy (he will do his best at imitating a high-pitched voice, but it is clear that he is unconvincing: line 268), and by showing every last detail of the process. Particularly striking is the singeing of his pubic hair in order to make a convincing woman of him (lines 236-48). This would clearly not be a necessary part of an actor's preparation to become a tragic character, and again it points to the difference between tragedy and comedy in respect of the body. Comedy is able to draw attention to genitals and even put males on stage wearing a comic leather *phallus*. But the audience cannot think of the actor's body beneath the costume in a tragedy, without the effect being spoiled. So, for example, when Clytemnestra begs her son Orestes, appealing by her breast, not to kill her in Aeschylus' *Libation Bearers* 896-8, it must be taken as more metaphorical than literal (it seems unlikely that the actor removes a fake breast from his costume and neither is the audience likely to think about the fact he is male, if they are properly engaged with the drama). Similarly, when Perseus falls madly in love with Andromeda when first catching sight of her in Euripides' *Andromeda* (now fragmentary; for a translation and discussion of the play see Collard et al. 2004, 133-68), there could be no hint of the actor beneath the female costume or the entire effect of the moment would be spoiled. Aristophanes is, then, playing a sophisticated game with his engagement in theatrical discourse here, since he is apparently deconstructing the processes behind theatre, but in fact is deliberately misrepresenting them in order to create humour. It also points to a difference between the costumes in both types of theatre: whereas comic costume can sometimes be transparent, tragic costume cannot. This comment, as with many comments relating to costume, is also more broadly applicable to the two approaches to theatre: comedy is far more direct and transparent, while tragedy remains more indirect and opaque.

Euripides responds to this scene, and the comment that Aristophanes makes through it, in his *Bacchae*, which was produced at some time after 408 BC. We have already seen how the religious insignia of Dionysus is set up by Euripides to be understood as analogous to theatre costume in that play (see Chapter 4). The expression of this idea finds its culmination in the dressing up of Pentheus himself in the costume of a maenad (Euripides, *Bacchae* 913f.). Even though the process of putting on the costume does not take place on stage, there is nevertheless a strong allusion to the Inlaw scene which invites the audience to interpret the presentation of Pentheus through the lens of that earlier comic scene. The inter-performative allusion is made through the verbal and visual echo of a detail in the earlier scene: Inlaw is concerned to arrange the pleats of the dress around his legs (line 256), and similarly both Dionysus and Pentheus will draw attention to whether Pentheus' dress pleats are in order (lines 935-8). So what is it that Euripides uses the allusion and the scene to say? It seems that he retaliates against Aristophanes' strategy for making the costuming process, and the creation of theatre, into something humorous,

99

by showing that in fact putting on costume could be deadly serious; even those elements which had been comic in the Aristophanic handling of it, like the fussing over pleats, could be made unfunny in Euripides' hands. The gravity of the situation in the *Bacchae* kills the comedy of the cross-dressing. The audience must know that this costume spells Pentheus' death, since Dionysus has said beforehand that he will put the finery on Pentheus which he will take as he goes to Hades (line 857). After these words have been spoken, the maenad dress becomes the equivalent of the death clothing which we have seen in operation in other tragedies (see Chapter 4), and the same Greek term is used to refer to it (*kosmos*). Euripides therefore exploits both the theatrical past and the concept of determinism to make this presentation of cross-dressing sinister and terrifying, as opposed to comic. The broader comment that he makes about theatre through this seems to be that tragedy and comedy may be based on the same theatrical processes (such as dressing up in costume), but in tragedy they are often used to create theatre which is serious and emotionally affecting, whereas in comedy they are used primarily to create humour. There is also perhaps here a response to Aristophanes' earlier implicit claim (in the *Acharnians*, see above) that comedy was the better genre through which to contribute to theatrical discourse since it could be more direct. Through this scene in the *Bacchae*, Euripides seems to be suggesting that in fact tragedy is better suited to comment on theatre, because it can do so seriously. For a different interpretation of the blurring of genres in this scene, see Foley (1980), who argues that the borrowing from comedy is for the sake of Dionysus displaying his divinity.

At the end of this line of the commentary on theatre taking place between tragedy and comedy in their handling of costume, is Aristophanes' *Frogs* in 405 BC. This comedy takes as its explicit theme the question of what makes a good tragedy, and it contains some of the best known comments on Euripides' use of costume: namely the criticism of his use of rags. It is important to see these comments both in light of the comments that had gone before and in the direct context of the play setting. We have already seen how Euripides had been associated with costume and its use to comment on theatre, in Aristophanic comedy: it is from him that Dicaeopolis will borrow the Telephus' costume in the *Acharnians* and it is in fact through his prompting, and for his sake, that Inlaw will get dressed up as a woman in the *Women at the Thesmophoria*. We have also seen how Euripides himself was concerned to comment on theatre through costume and engaged in a dialogue on this basis with Aristophanes through their respective plays. It is hardly surprising then, that in a comedy which is pre-occupied with the question of tragedy's purpose and how best to create it, attention should be given to Euripides' use of costume. Twenty years of theatre later, Aristophanes picks up where he left off in his criticism of Euripidean rags in the *Acharnians*, only here the criticism is put in the mouth of the character Aeschylus who in this comedy is trying to prove that he is a better tragedian than Euripides. The context and details of the criticism are important to understanding exactly what is being asserted about Euripidean dramaturgy and theatre in general.

Aeschylus, who in this play and debate is characterised as a traditionalist, criticises Euripides' use of rag-costumes in two parts of the comedy (Aristophanes, *Frogs* 840-6, tr. Sommerstein 1996; my emphasis):

> **Aeschylus** How dare you, you son of that goddess of the vegetable-plot? *You* say that of *me*, you scraper-together of idle chatter, you *creator of beggars*, you *stitcher of rags*? You're going to be sorry you did!
> **Dionysus** Stop now, Aeschylus, 'heat not thine inward parts with wrathful ire'.
> **Aeschylus** No, I *won't* stop, not till I've thoroughly shown up this *creator of cripples* for what he is, in spite of all his effrontery.

Later in the debate, he returns to this criticism (Aristophanes, *Frogs* 1058-68, tr. Sommerstein 1996):

> **Aeschylus** It's absolutely imperative, you wretched fool, when expressing great thoughts and ideas, to create words that measure up to them. And anyway, it's only natural that the demigods should use words bigger than ours, just as they wear much more splendid clothes than we do – something in which I set a good example that you utterly perverted.
> **Euripides** By doing what?
> **Aeschylus** In the first place by dressing men of kingly station in rags, so as to make people see them as objects of pity.
> **Euripides** So did I do any harm by that?
> **Aeschylus** Well, for a start, thanks to that, there isn't one rich man who's willing to take charge of a warship. Instead he wraps himself in rags and wails and claims to be poor.
> **Dionysus** When all the time, by Demeter, he's got a fleecy woollen tunic underneath! And if he hoodwinks them successfully with that tale, up he pops next moment around the fishmongers' stalls!

In the first passage, Euripides' excessive use of the character-in-rags device is criticised, as it had been in the *Acharnians*. The difference is that while in the *Acharnians* the criticism was presented through a farce which gently mocked this apparent characteristic, here in the mouth of the character Aeschylus it comes in the form of an accusation and offers the basis for a stream of abuse. What is it that is apparently so offensive to Aeschylus about the excessive use of rags by Euripides? The second passage unravels some of the reasoning behind Aeschylus' position. There are two separate explanations given for why he is so against Euripides' costuming strategies. The first is his assertion that demigods should be dressed like demigods and that, therefore, kings should be dressed like kings and not made pitiable by being presented in rags. The second objection is that Euripides' costuming strategies have taught a dangerous lesson in *mimesis* (imitation), so that the rich citizens of Athens, copying what they have seen in his plays, now dress up in rags in order to pretend they are poor and to avoid making financial contributions to the city. This second objection is perhaps not intended by Aristophanes to be taken as seriously by the audience in terms of the theatrical discourse that he is setting out through this debate. It is a joke, of particularly dark humour, which alludes to the reality of the contemporary poverty in Athens after years of the city being at war. It is designed to make light of a reality and offer reassurance by fantasising that, in fact, the elite's loss of wealth was only a pretence. Alternatively, if there really was a group of the elite who were engaged in the equivalent of tax evasion, then the humour here must be in the suggestion that this could be entirely down to Euripides! In fact, of course, following Aeschylus' logic, Aristophanes himself was just as culpable, if not more so, in this respect, since he had offered the model to the citizens for the 'adopt a rag costume from Euripidean drama' ruse; in effect, Dicaeopolis in the *Acharnians* can be argued to be responsible for giving the citizens this idea. The awareness of this and the sense of irony that it creates in this joke, makes it clear that this part of the objection is not meant as a serious criticism against the Euripidean way of doing drama in particular; after all, since the core of the accusation is based on the dangers of *mimesis* (the citizens could learn how to get dressed up and pretend to be someone else from any drama), it could be turned back against Aeschylus or any playwright, and therefore only serves to show how ridiculous and extreme the character of Aeschylus is in this play.

The first objection is more interesting in what it reveals about the underlying theatrical discourse with which Aristophanes is engaging in this play. Aeschylus claims that his problem with Euripides' costuming is that characters are not dressed as they should be, or rather that his costumes do not always reflect the status of the characters who wear them. The extreme example he gives of this is a king dressed in rags. The real-life Aeschylus had himself presented a king dressed in rags in his tragedy *Persians*, where Xerxes returns from his campaign against Greece with his finery in tatters (see Chapter 3). So this objection needs to be recognised as representative not of the real-life Aeschylus' view, but of the tradition-alist stance which his character in this play embodies. There must have been at least some portion of Athenian society who held this stance, otherwise the play would lose its dramatic point and relevance. So what is at the core of this objection? The problem is that with this system of costuming it is not easy to determine the status of a character from the semiotics of his or her costume. Instead of communicating identity or status, the costume communicates the state the characters are in. This implies a more complex type of dramaturgy than the one advocated by the traditionalist ideal of 'demigods should dress like demigods'. But the traditionalist's anxiety does not seem to be rooted in the concern that this approach to costuming makes watching drama more of the challenge. It is rather that it is unsettling to be presented with a type of costuming strategy that breaks with a simplistic system where costume acted as a clear semiotic indicator of status. Under this alternative system, it is no longer possible to know from external signs who people are and where they stand in society.

This anxiety was clearly one dominating late fifth-century society where changes in circumstances were making it increasingly difficult to rely on semiotic indications in order to determine someone's status. According to the fifth-century writer known as the Old Oligarch, it was impossible to tell the difference between slaves and citizens in Athens since they dressed in the same way (Pseudo-Xenophon, *Constitution of the Athenians* 1.10). This may be an exaggeration on the part of this writer, but it reflects some kind of reality or at least current concern within the society. Moreover the plays of Euripides himself frequently reflect a related concern about the difficulty of telling whether someone is good or bad from his/her external appearance. The vehemence of the objection against Euripides' costuming approach therefore seems to be a reflection of the traditionalist anxiety over the blurring of boundaries in real-life society. The insistence that theatre should maintain the rule of correspondence between costume and status implies a belief that somehow controlling the system of semiotics on stage could have an impact on the situation in society. The logic of this makes more sense when viewed in the context of the assertion made earlier in the play, and just before this passage, that tragedy should provide teaching to the citizens of Athens (Aristophanes, *Frogs* 1009-10 and 1053-6). So that, the costuming strategies of a playwright are understood to be indicative of the type of theatre which he is producing and what he is teaching through that theatrical experience at the same time. The joke about rich men putting on rags to fake poverty, though primarily humorous, in fact also functions to reinforce this idea that tragedy's costuming has the potential to teach something; in the joke we see the evidence of this in a practical example. Costume, and its semiotic deployment in the plays, forms a major part of the debate about theatre which is presented in the *Frogs*. It is not only apparent from this that costume can be used as a symbolic way of talking about the creation of theatre but also that discussing alternative costuming strategies can be a means to set out ideas on the purpose of theatre and the right way to do it.

Looking beyond the fifth century, costume continues to offer a means of representing and exploring tragic theatre, and retains a central place in theatrical discourse. This is apparent both from visual and textual evidence. In terms of visual evidence, the representation of the Muse of Tragedy, Melpomene, tells a revealing story. From perhaps as early as the Hellenistic period and certainly by the first century BC, Melpomene is often represented wearing pieces of Heracles' costume (see Wyles 2007, 170-2). So, for example, she might be shown wearing his lion skin and carrying his club and tragic mask. Melpomene is represented in this way on coins, in wall paintings, and in statuary (see *LIMC* 7 (supplement) 'Mousa, Mousai/Musae'). Her appearance in this guise on small pieces as well as more prominent ones, in public and private contexts, suggests that it was a widespread and familiar way of representing her. We have already seen in Chapter 4 how Heracles' costume had been used by Aristophanes in the *Frogs* as a means through which to invite the audience to think about how costume works to create character. This theatrical treatment of Heracles' costume added another layer to its meaning and gave it the potential to become a symbol for the process by which costume transforms actors into characters and theatre is created. It is hardly surprising, then, to find that Melpomene, the Muse of Tragedy, is shown dressed in *his* costume. She represents the tragic art and fundamental to that art is the creation of theatre through dressing up in costume. As a way of drawing attention to that statement, she is dressed in Heracles' costume which was already, after *Frogs*, a short-hand for one of the processes that lay behind tragedy. It is also possible that her appearance in tragic costume is meant to draw attention to the idea, also engaged with by Aristophanes in the tragedian scenes in *Acharnians* and *Women at the Thesmophoria*, that the composition of tragedy (another essential process behind its creation) was inspired by costume. Since the Muses traditionally offer inspiration to the authors writing in their genre, it is all the more fitting that Melpomene, as the inspiration of tragedians should be represented carrying pieces of costume. Costume as representative of the artform of tragedy, as well as perhaps a symbol of an individual play, is also evidenced in a marble relief dating to the second century BC and now held in Istanbul's Archaeological Museum (no. 1242; see Bieber 1961, fig. 109). The relief shows Euripides passing a tragic mask to the personification of the Stage (*skene*) while Dionysus looks on. The idea is that what Euripides produces and puts on stage can be embodied by the tragic mask; all the processes of composition and theatre-creation are represented by this single piece of costume. Again, this corresponds to a point made by Aristophanes in his engagement with theatrical discourse, as in the *Acharnians* the costumes surrounding Euripides are understood to represent and embody whole plays (see Macleod 1974).

Textual evidence too supports the emerging picture of the place that costume held in the landscape of cultural thinking about theatre. Plutarch, writing in the first/second century AD, offers a striking description of the process of creating tragedy (Plutarch, *On the Fame of the Athenians* 6 = *Moralia* 348e-f, tr. Babbit 1936):

> Let their [the poets'] tragic actors accompany them, men like Nicostratus and Callipides, Mynniscus, Theodorus, and Polus, who robe Tragedy and bear her litter, as though she were some woman of wealth; or rather, let them follow on as though they were painters and gilders and dyers of statues.

In this description of creating tragic theatre, the actors are described as figuratively dressing the female personification of Tragedy. The dressing of Tragedy needs to be understood as analogous to the actor's process of putting on a costume, which as we have already seen could stand for the creation of theatre in theatrical discourse. So in a very self-reflexive way, dressing up Tragedy becomes a means of symbolising the creation of tragic theatre on stage. Her clothing, just as Heracles' costume on Melpomene, stands for both what tragedy is and how it is created. This suggests that costume continued to be an easy means through which to think about theatre.

Finally, an anecdote about a tragic performance in the first century AD reveals a mentality which equated understanding tragedy with understanding costume, and therefore implies that costume could somehow stood for the whole of the tragic art. The anecdote is recorded in a fragment of the historian Eunapius, who was writing in the fourth century AD and therefore over 300 years after this alleged performance. So while it is not sure evidence for this mentality about costume in the first century, it certainly reveals that it is still around in the fourth century AD and in fact, the other evidence that we have looked at suggests that this is a continuation of a type of conceptual thinking which had already been current in society. The anecdote is told as follows (tr. Möllendorff 2001, 124-5):

> It is said that something similar happened in Nero's reign, but in one whole city. For they say that a certain tragic actor, having been exiled from Rome on account of Nero's own ambitions in this area, decided to go off <to ...> and to exhibit his outstanding voice to men who were half-barbarian; and he came to this great and populous city and invited them to the theatre. When they gathered on the first day the performance was a failure, since the audience could not endure the sight, which they saw for the first time, but fled, crushing and trampling each other in the process. But when the actor had taken the leading men aside and showed them the nature of the mask and the boots which increased his height impressively, he persuaded them in this way to endure the sight and he came on stage again.

The anecdote goes on to explain that this second attempt is a greater success and the audience is spell-bound by the power of the performance. The point here is that the actor goes to perform to a people who have no experience of tragic performance and before they can accept or understand it, he has to explain elements of his costume. Although on the surface the explanation of it is deemed necessary because the mask and height of the boots (Roman tragic costume was more exaggerated in these respects: see Chapter 1), make the actor a terrifying sight, there is also an implicit logic to this explanation. What it seems to suggest is that those who are inexperienced in the tragic art, must understand and accept costume before they can enjoy it. The costume has to be explained to the leading men and then when the actor comes on the second time he will employ techniques to introduce the audience gradually to the range of voice used in performance, but it is the costume above all which needs to be understood first. This suggests the privileged place which costume continued to hold in the ancient view of theatre and how it worked; costume, and its acceptance, is fundamental to appreciating the artform and it could therefore frequently take the role of symbolising the theatrical experience. We will look at the development of this idea further in the next chapter.

Internalised comments on costume within the plays have the potential to invite reflection not only on theatre costume, but also, more broadly, on theatre itself. Through analysing the treatment of costume, we can therefore come to a closer understanding of the fifth-century playwrights' thoughts about theatre and how it operated. Knowledge of this theoretical thinking has the obvious advantage of enabling a more informed assessment of the dramatic techniques exploited in their plays and the likely audience response to them (given the impact of this discourse). Beyond theatre in general, an examination of the discourse also reveals something about the understanding of generic boundaries between tragedy and comedy, and serves to remind us that these were by no means yet fixed in the fifth century (as the competitiveness over which genre is fittest to contribute to theatrical discourse shows). As a consequence of this long-lasting and closely involved use of costume in fifth-century drama, costume was established as the central symbol, or thinking space, within theatrical discourse for centuries afterwards.

Translating Costume across Cultures

In the last chapter we were looking at costume's status as a symbol through which to represent theatre or through which to explore the theatrical art. This status, established by fifth-century playwrights' manipulation of costume in their engagement with a shared theatrical discourse, extended well beyond the fifth century BC and carried over into Roman culture. While this remained a constant, other aspects of the way in which tragic costume was approached and understood changed. One difference has already been hinted at in the anecdote about a tragic performance given to a city of half-barbarians during Nero's rule (see the end of Chapter 5). The audience is, at first, terrified by the sight of the tragic actor because of his high boots and mask (see Fig. 15). The extremities that the material appearance of costume had reached in the Roman period necessarily elicited different responses and attitudes towards it. Lucian, the second-century AD writer, for example, could present the tragic costume as truly grotesque in his defence of pantomime dancing, where he says (Lucian, *On the Dance* 27, tr. Fowler and Fowler 1905):

> In forming our estimate of tragedy, let us first consider its externals – the hideous, appalling spectacle that the actor presents. His high boots raise him up out of all proportion; his head is hidden under an enormous mask; his huge mouth gapes upon the audience as if he would swallow them; to say nothing of the chest-pads and stomach-pads with which he contrives to give himself an artificial corpulence, lest his deficiency in this respect should emphasise his disproportionate height.

What this passage reveals is the possibility of assessing the whole artform on the basis of its visual appearance – so that the changes to the costume by the time of the Roman period could actually have implications for the cultural attitude towards tragedy. The passage, though, must of course be understood in context. Lucian's overall purpose in this treatise is to argue in favour of pantomime dance which was the ancient equivalent of ballet: a single performer danced the story from myth (often covering tragic material), taking all the roles, to the accompaniment of music. Lucian uses the comparison with tragic performance in order to praise pantomime; so here he emphasises the grotesqueness of tragic costume to show how beautiful the pantomime dancer's appearance is by contrast. For each aspect of tragic costume criticised here, the pantomime dancer's costume is directly the opposite. The high boots, gaping mask and padding of tragic costume contrasts with the flat sandals, closed-mouth mask, and slinky diaphanous silk costume of the pantomime dancer; on the pantomime dancer's costume, see Wyles (2008). There is therefore naturally some deliberate exaggeration here and tragic costume is being presented in a particular way for the sake of Lucian's overall purpose. Nevertheless, the anecdote about the response of the half-barbarian city to the tragic performer (see Chapter 5) confirms how striking the appearance of tragic costume was by this time and this is supported further by the visual evidence (see Chapter 1).

The appearance of tragic costume, and responses to it, could be presented in a more positive way in other contexts. So, even Lucian himself is capable of taking a very different approach to it, which instead of characterising the costume as hideous or ridiculous, treats it as something grand and worthy of respect. In another of his works, he describes it as follows (Lucian, *Wisdom of Nigrinus* 11, tr. Harman 1936):

> Time and again when they [actors] have assumed the role of Agamemnon or Creon or even Heracles himself, costumed in cloth of gold with fierce eyes and mouths agape, they speak in a voice that is small, thin, womanish, and far too poor for Hecuba or Polyxena. Therefore to avoid being criticised like them for wearing a mask altogether too big for my head and for being a disgrace to my costume, I want to talk to you with my features exposed, so that the hero whose part I am taking may not be brought down with me if I stumble.

The metaphor employed here carries an implicit criticism of actors who are not good enough to play the tragic roles they attempt. The idea is that the costume, rather than being hideous, is something magnificent with its gold cloth and huge fierce mask. The actor who is unable to muster the stage presence demanded by the costume risks being a disgrace to it; which is the metaphorical consequence that the interlocutor wishes to avoid. Clearly costume by this point had become more exaggerated in its appearance, but the attitude taken towards it depends on the context in which it is being viewed or discussed (on Lucian and tragic costume see Kokolakis 1961).

These passages also draw attention to a shift in the conceptualisation of tragic costume. The costume is presented as belonging to the actor rather than to any particular character. In the passage from the *Wisdom of Nigrinus* (above), the actor is described as adopting the gold cloth costume and the fierce mask whether he is playing Agamemnon or Creon or Heracles. There is not the same sense, as there was in the fifth century (see Chapter 4), that a costume belonged to a specific character, and the language of costume in Roman performances did not have all the same possibilities for creating meaning. The tragic costume seems to have come to define primarily the performer rather than the character, i.e. it communicated that the person on stage was a tragic actor, before the role which he was playing. In part this shift must be put down to the difference of performance context between fifth-century Athens and Imperial Rome. Tragedy in Rome was one of many different entertainments put on stage and therefore there was perhaps a greater demand for the costume to suggest the type of performer before anything else. In fact, the types of theatre in Rome could be classified by the dress or footwear characteristically worn by the actors: so that the term 'fabula palliata', i.e. a play performed in the *pallium* (a typically Greek garment), could be used to designate a Roman adaptation based on a Greek original, while a 'fabula togata' (suggesting actors were costumed in the *toga*) referred to native drama (see Appendix D in Beare 1950). In such a system of classification, the costume is, above all, a signifier of the type of play which is being performed; secondarily it may communicate something about the particular character being presented. The priorities in the audience's reading of the costume, therefore, must shift together with the general attitude towards costume and its place in the cultural imagination. The semiotic status of the tragic boots is closely related to this general shift in approach to tragic costume. In fifth-century Athens, tragic footwear might be relevant to characterisation (see Chapter 4) but did not carry significance beyond this (i.e. as a generic marker). By the time of the Roman Empire, it was a different story. Tragic boots were not only far more striking in appearance with their platform heels (see above and Chapter 1), but they also carried a special symbolic status. The tragic boots (*cothurni*) now held the place of representing the tragic artform, and much as the mask with down-turned mouth in modern times, offered an easy symbolic short-hand for tragedy (see, for example, Horace, *On the Art of Poetry* 80).

As well as a shift in the appearance of costume and how it was conceptualised, there was also necessarily a change to the range of its possible meanings. This comes about because each society reads the signs, or visual information, making up a costuming strategy, in a different way. The visual landscape of the average audience member in Imperial Rome was very different from that of a fifth-century Athenian spectator. It is not just a question of the appearance of the city (its architecture and public monuments, etc.), but also exposure to newly-developed or culture-specific performance arts, as well as an inevitable shift in emphasis on signs which had particular prominence in the society. This difference in visual experience means that the way in which the audience responds to costume and reads semiotics, is just not the same. To give an example of a sign that would be responded to differently, we could think about the beard on Heracles' mask. This is illustrated on the mask held in the hand by the actor on the Pronomos vase (Fig. 9b). The representation of the beard on the mask seems to have remained constant throughout antiquity (see Wyles 2007, 231), so that we can be confident that the Roman audience is faced with a similar visual set of data. In fifth-century Athens, the beard would merely communicate the maturity of this hero. But the symbolic significance of the beard would be different to a Roman audience. In Rome, a full beard like this was associated with the society's unsophisticated past (see, for example, Cicero, *Pro Caelio* 33). On the visual level too, the audience would probably have gained experience of such beards in the representation of the men of the past at funerals in the procession of the *imagines* (portrait masks of ancestors) which must have reinforced the association (see Wyles 2007, 232-3). This type of beard was also closely associated with the great men of fifth-century Greece, including the tragic poets who continued to be depicted with serious beards in the iconographic tradition. So in the time of Augustus, for example, this beard on the tragic mask of Heracles not only said something about the hero's age but also had the semiotic potential to place him as a figure among the men of Roman society's past or even fifth-century Greece. The full beard would only come back into fashion in the second century, under the influence of the phil-hellenic Hadrian, and this in turn would alter perceptions of the mask, and by extension the tragic hero, making him suddenly rather contemporary. The Roman audience, whether before or after Hadrian, come to Heracles' beard with an existing association and prejudice which inform their response to it.

This same observation applies across all the semiotic pieces making up the language of costume – they simply cannot be read or experienced in exactly the same way as they had been in Athens. Even if an identical costume were used in the performance of a revival or an adaptation of a fifth-century Greek tragedy, the meaning it produced would be different. It is not just a question of the new associations which the Roman audience brings to reading costume, but also the more specific associations which may have been lost. So, for example, in the visual landscape of Athenian culture, the snake had a special and prominent position since it was sacred to Athena, the patron goddess of the city, and was often associated with her in iconography; for example a huge golden snake was incorporated into the design of the Athena Parthenos statue on the Acropolis. Euripides recognises this and exploits its dramatic potential in his *Ion*, where the golden snake necklace (Euripides, *Ion* 1427-31), which is one of the items to enable the long-awaited recognition between Creusa and Ion, would resonate in a very particular way with Athenian spectators and clearly would not have the same impact in a performance outside that city. This is just one example of a symbol which would have resonated differently, but there must be many others. Some elements of the semiotics in tragic costume are culturally specific and in this sense their visual meaning is topical; they may appear in the vocabulary of another society's stage language but they do not communicate the same thing. If we take, for example, the use of black for mourning in Greece, Rome and our society, while this is a semiotic overlap and, broadly speaking, a shared symbol of grief, nevertheless the other layers of association to that symbol will differ in each cultural context (since it depends on the unique cluster of ideas, customs, and processes associated with death in each). The three audiences read the tragic costume presented to them on the basis of a different set of visual experiences and semiotic assumptions.

This difference, however, was not necessarily recognised by the Roman audience who may, in fact, have approached tragedy with the expectation that they were watching something 'authentic'. This idea is certainly encouraged by the continuity suggested in Augustan writers (for example, Horace, *On the Art of Poetry* 275-80, tr. Rudd 1997):

> We are told Thespis discovered the genre of the tragic Muse which was never known before; he carried his plays on a wagon to be sung and acted by men who had smeared lees on their faces. After him came Aeschylus, introducing the mask and lordly robe; he laid a stage on lowish supports and called for a sonorous diction and the wearing of high-soled boots.

Horace's comment invites his contemporary reader to imagine that the tragic performances in Rome, and specifically the use of boots in the costuming, reflected the performance practice of fifth-century Athens. This claim is made in other sources too which help to keep the tradition alive (see Appendix). But in fact, Roman tragic costume, as we have seen in Chapter 1, was materially very different from what had been in use in the fifth century. The only possible similarity was the belted, long-sleeved, long *chiton* worn by the tragic actor – but even this was not the 'same' costume, in the sense that it would not carry the same symbolic associations for the two audiences. The sleeves of the costume, for example, had a specific semiotic association in fifth-century Athens which could enable them, through the model of the past as a foreign country, to suggest the mythological time setting of the plays (see Chapter 4). The sleeves could not operate within this same system of thinking in Rome and so meant something different to the spectator. Elements of the costume which remained materially the same were not, therefore, necessarily semiotic equivalents. The surprising thing is that some of the materially furthest removed elements of later tragic costume, which on the surface do not seem to have a connection to the fifth century, can in fact prove to be the ones which are closest in terms of the effect that they produce. If we think again about the tragic boots and the use of platform heels on them in the Roman period, they may in fact offer a semiotic equivalent to the sleeves in ancient Greece. Although the material evidence shows Horace's scheme of Aeschylus introducing the heeled *cothurni* to be fictional, the important factor, in terms of semiotics, is not the historical truth of the boots' performance history, but the audience's perception of it. If the Roman audience believed that such boots had been used in fifth-century Athens, then the boots become capable of representing and suggesting the past. In this sense, the boots function as semiotic equivalents in Roman performances to the sleeves in the fifth century BC.

The idea of 'translating' costume, or a costuming strategy, therefore is a highly complex process, since it is not just a set of material objects that is being translated but a network of semiotic meanings. Many of the observations just made about the issues surrounding the approach to tragic costume in the Roman period hold good for performances in other periods and societies too. One of the greatest challenges to a production must be to find semiotic equivalents to the costuming of the tragedies, if this performance element is to produce the same experience or effect on the audience. Modern performances which opt for authentic-looking or ancient costume are in one sense being true to the original, but at the same time this costuming strategy can produce a very different theatrical experience from the fifth-century première. The problem is that using ancient-style costume can sidestep the issue of translating the symbolism of the costumes and its dramatic effects, at the same time as introducing an overall effect which elicits a different response from the original. Most obviously, the 'authentic' Greek-style costume in modern productions cannot have the same significance or meaning to the modern audience as it did in the original performance context. The modern audience is operating in a different world in terms of semiotic codes; therefore elements of the costume which would be easy to read for the original audience pose a challenge now. The line of Western theatre history and its inheritance from ancient theatre have made some of the techniques of the language of costume and its manipulation in Greek tragedy familiar. But despite this, the language of tragic costume operates on the basis of a mostly alien semiotic code, and the audience confronted with ancient costume may therefore often find themselves in the position of Pelasgus in Aeschylus' *Suppliants*: wondering how to interpret the costume and determine its meaning (see Chapter 3). This clearly changes the status of the costume as a sign in the performance, since it now becomes a symbol for obscured or indecipherable meaning. Authentic costume is fundamentally limited in what it is able to communicate to a modern audience. What it says to the audience, above all, is that they are watching a play set in the past of ancient Greece, distant from our contemporary world and alien to it.

As a secondary, and perhaps not so crucial, consideration, the quality of the tragedy's time setting is fundamentally changed by a modern performance using ancient costumes. Since although the costumes of such a production will suggest a setting in the past, it will not be the same kind of past as we saw being created on the fifth-century stage. In Athenian productions, we saw how foreign elements could suggest that the action on the stage was taking place at some point in Greece's past (see Chapter 4). At the same time, this mythological past world of the play is rather fluid (since it is constructed rather than strictly historical); it is possible for the costume to invite the audience to bring the contemporary world into their vision (see Chapter 4 on Heracles' breastplate). What happens when a modern production uses ancient costumes? It creates a past which is in comparison rather one-dimensional. Unless the performance is in Greece, it is unlikely that the audience will have a sense of viewing their own past (even when the debt of our cultural heritage to ancient Greece is acknowledged). The modern audience may judge from the costuming that a play is set in either ancient Greece or the mythological past – there is not the sense of distinction between the two and so the rich texture and complexity of the time-setting created through the costume in the original is lost. Related to this is the issue of how distant the action of the play seems to be from the audience's own world. In ancient Greece the occasional hints of the present in the costuming (or the potential of it) keep the playworld from seeming too distant from the spectators. But in the modern production, the authentic costume is fundamentally alien and therefore keeps the audience at a distance from the play. This might have its own dramatic effect and value, but it creates a different experience from that of the costume in ancient productions.

In fact, there are two different possible approaches to adopting 'ancient' costume in a production, and each creates a different experience for the audience. A production is either committed to being as historically accurate as possible in its costuming or it uses costumes which simply cohere to the audience's notion of ancient theatre costume (or even ancient Greek dress); both approaches are using 'authentic' costume, each in its own sense. A part of the purpose of Chapter 1 was to dispel the misconceptions about fifth-century tragic costume and above all the stereotype of the notorious white bedsheet. The survey of the visual evidence shows a much wider range of costume design being used. But for many audiences, costumes made up of draped white fabric will immediately suggest a setting in ancient Greece and therefore, from this point of view, the 'authentic' choice of costuming is in fact the historically inaccurate one; just as in ancient Rome the high-soled boots seem the authentic footwear for tragedy. The problem with this is that while the costume communicates the setting clearly, it is perhaps nòt possible for it to be used to the same effect as it had been in the original play. The director or costume designer is therefore faced with the challenge of balancing what is more important in terms of the production's impact. On the other hand, there is little point in a production trying to make costume as accurate as possible, according to the material discussed in Chapter 1, if this is going to mean less to the audience and fail to suggest anything other than an alien world; the inflexible limitation is that the semiotic sign can only have significance within the framework of the audience's knowledge.

Unappealing as it may seem to a modern perspective to prize historical accuracy above all else in costuming (see comments of Llewellyn-Jones 2001), there was in fact a phase in theatre history, and in the story of the productions of ancient drama, when this was the primary concern (for an overview of the performance of ancient drama from the Renaissance on, see Bieber 1961, 254-7). One example of such a project in British theatre history is the Reading School Greek play which was first put on in 1806 and gained such a reputation for its accuracy that in 1821 its costumes could be praised as 'exact' (see Hall and Macintosh 2005, 261-2). The Reading School productions foreshadowed the movement towards historical accuracy in costume design which developed later in the same century in the 1880s (see Hall and Macintosh 2005, 477-9). This concern for historical accuracy is in fact out of keeping with the fifth-century Athenian approach to tragedy, which as we have seen took a fluid approach to the past constructed on the stage and had little concern for anachronism. In contrast, a performance aiming for precise historical accuracy becomes a different kind of exercise, which, delighting in erudition and the game of historical reconstruction (see below, comments of Sheridan Morley on Hall's *Oresteia*), limits the meaning of the costume to the audience. In these cases the effective communication of the costuming as a semiotic strategy is not a primary interest.

However 'exact' the costume of the Reading School Greek play might have seemed at the time, historical accuracy depends on the status of archaeological findings and the general state of knowledge at any given period. The comment about the Reading play's costumes being 'exact' may have seemed a fair assessment in 1821, but twenty years later the first engraving of the Pronomos vase, found in 1835, would be published (see Lissarrague 2010, 35), and change the picture of authentic ancient theatre costume (see Fig. 9). Ironically one of the most striking reproductions or imitations of ancient tragic costume was not intended for stage at all, but made its appearance as an evening dress in Madeleine Vionnet's haute couture Winter collection for 1921. The dress (Fig. 20) copies its motifs and pattern from the costumes of the actor on the Pronomos vase (Fig. 9b). While the design was acknowledged to take its inspiration from a Greek vase, the dress was not an attempt to replicate fifth-century tragic costume and certainly the fabrication is far from authentic (it is made of crêpe and patterned with beadwork sewn with gold thread). Furthermore, its colouring in orange with blue/black patterning has more to do with the red-figure vase which inspires it than ancient tragic costume. Nevertheless, the connection between the dress and ancient theatre costume is instantly striking to anyone familiar with the Pronomos vase. What is so telling, however, is that to most viewers the dress bears no relation to the costumes of ancient Greek drama at all. This highlights that while accuracy might be dependent on the state of archaeological knowledge, the idea of what looks authentic depends on the prevalent notions about ancient tragic costume. Paradoxically, the most accurate rendering of Greek tragic costume, based on all the currently available visual evidence, could seem far from authentic to the modern audience. In fact, in the most extreme case, for someone familiar with the Vionnet dress before the Pronomos vase, a production with costumes based on it would perhaps more readily suggest haute couture than the world of ancient Greek drama! Any

Fig. 20. Vionnet's 'Greek vase' evening dress, 1921.

costuming strategy cannot escape the existing associations of the audience and the implications which these semiotic givens will have for how the costume is understood.

Peter Hall's *Oresteia*, produced at the National Theatre in 1981, offers an excellent case example for the kinds of responses and problems that attempted authenticity can provoke. We should be clear that the production was not concerned in the same way as some of the nineteenth-century productions, referred to above, with absolute historical accuracy according to the archaeological evidence. The costumes found a happy compromise by incorporating elements which suggested ancient Greece (e.g. the breastplate and helmet of Agamemnon) without sacrificing meaning to historical exactness. So, for example, the costume used for Cassandra, the Trojan prophetess, gave a sense of her ethnic difference (especially through its fabric and the headdress; see Fig. 21), but it did not incorporate any authentic strong 'foreign' marker from ancient performance practice, like the floppy *kidaris* (on which see Chapter 4), which risked meaning little to the audience.

But there was an authentic element to the costuming which sparked controversy at the time: the masks worn by the entire male cast (see Fig. 21). These masks, made of muslin and plaster of Paris and designed by Jocelyn Herbert, were not intended to be strictly historically exact but their use was nevertheless perceived as an indulgent academic exercise of limited theatrical meaning. Milton Shulman (*The Standard*, 30 November 1981), refers to the production as an 'experiment for classical scholars' and for Michael Billington, too, it seemed that the director had put intellectual interest above theatre; after acknowledging that there were good reasons to use masks in ancient performances, he concludes (*The Guardian*, 30 November 1981):

> To employ them today (whatever the intellectual motive) seems to me as perverse as making a movie without sound or doing Shakespeare in a mock-Elizabethan playhouse. What was an accepted convention for the Greeks for us becomes an arty device.

Also firmly against the masks was Sheridan Morley (*Punch*, 9 December 1981):

> It is an academic experiment of considerable tedium, largely because for better or for worse we have now come to expect more of actors than movements of the voice and arms: we need eyebrows and eyes and cheeks and chins and mouths not frozen in immobility, and without that kind of life and detail we are left with a carefully choreographed museum display of what Greek drama might have looked like to the Greeks, one which not even the brilliance of Harrison's language and a stunning Harrison Birtwhistle score can bring to anything more than very occasional flashes of life.

Fig. 21. Cassandra and the chorus in Peter Hall's *Oresteia*.

One of the central problems of using this authentic piece of costuming is the shift in ways of viewing which have taken place in society and the change in performance tradition which leave modern audiences with a different set of semiotic expectations. A spectator in the theatre now, as Morley points out, is accustomed to reading the face as part of the semiotic process of interpreting the visual signs of a performance. It is therefore a strange experience to watch a production where the faces are fixed in 'immobility' through the use of mask. For some, this strangeness led to a feeling of alienation from the action; Michael Billington (see above) explains this effect of the masks in the first two plays (he is more positive about their use in the *Eumenides*): 'But in the earlier plays the masks so distance the spectator (this spectator anyway) as to leave him detached and unfeeling.' The problem is that the mask now creates a distance that it is unlikely to have in the original, where the use of mask was a more culturally familiar activity (see Halliwell 1993). The masks were also criticised for the way in which they imposed the personalities of the characters; Milton Shulman (see above) commented: 'Jocelyn Herbert's masks not only convert the entire cast into gesticulating puppets but force personalities upon the main characters which are disconcerting and inconsistent.' Again, this issue arises from different ways of viewing and expectations of drama; the power of elements of costume to 'transform' the actor or impose personality was clearly not such a disturbing prospect to the ancient mindset (see Chapter 4).

The final criticism of the masks was on a practical level since some complained that they muffled the actors' voices; even Benedict Nightingale, who is more positive about their use in general (see below) admits that the sound was muffled and John Barber (*The Daily Telegraph*, 30 November 1981) also comments on this. Again, this was not a problem experienced in the ancient performances, where we know that not only every word, but even every syllable could be clearly deciphered; this is shown in the anecdote about Hegelochus who, performing Euripides' *Orestes*, mispronounced an accent in line 279, so that he was understood to say that he could see a 'weasel', rather than a 'calm', coming after the storm (see Euripides, *Orestes* 279 and Aristophanes, *Frogs* 303-4). Both the issue of the alienating effect of the mask and its muffling of the sound fundamentally arise out of putting an authentic or ancient element into a new performance context. It may have seemed to some like an experiment for classical scholars, but in fact it offers some fascinating material for the analysis of theatre semiotics and the issues of translating costume strategies from one culture into another.

As a semiotic experiment, the use of the masks and the nod to ancient performance conventions were not universally criticised. Benedict Nightingale (*New Statesman*, 4 December 1981) even deemed the masks a part of the success:

> It's mostly terrific to look at and thanks to Harrison Birtwhistle's suggestive music and some careful exploitation of silence, splendidly atmospheric too. Jocelyn Herbert's masks are part of this success. They graphically remind us that the characters are elemental, not psychological beings; and they can also be wonderfully ambiguous, visibly altering according to the mood of the speaker, so that one moment the Furies boggle with incredulity, the next balefully seethe.

For him the masks were not frozen or immobile but shifted according to the body language of the actor. We can imagine how Cassandra's mask might convey a different mood from that of the performance still (Fig. 21) if the actor shifted his stance. Equally the masks of the chorus in the same shot do not all suggest the same feeling, but since the performers hold their heads at different angles, their similar masks create a variety of emotions. The potential of the mask in this respect has been shown by the works (practical and published) of the modern mask-maker, theatre practitioner, and classical scholar, Chris Vervain. Nightingale also identifies the helpfulness of the masks in directing the audience to view the characters as elemental, rather than psychological. While it might be 'correct' to view the characters in this way, the other reviews demonstrate how unnatural and difficult it is to unlearn what is now the natural way of constructing character (i.e. as psychological beings), and this in part explains the negative response to the masks. Oswyn Murray, a classical scholar, claimed that the effect of the use of men and the masks had erroneously been labelled 'alienation', and that, in fact, it universalised the action (*Times Literary Supplement*, 11 December 1981). Even if the masks did catapult the action onto the level of the universal, the relevance or impact of that action was limited by the fact that, as seems clear from most of the reviews, the effect of the masks *was* alienating for many.

The final advantage of the masks is one that was again difficult to appreciate in the context of our performance culture. In Chapter 4 we saw how the ancient use of masks had the advantage of giving the costume autonomy from the actor playing the part. The character's presence depends on the clothing, props, and mask, and the actor does not come into it. In unmasked theatre, however, the audience's knowledge of the actor's private life and past performances can affect their assessment of the character played (see Quinn 1990). Despite this potential advantage of the masks, the anonymity of the actors behind the characters was, in fact, another difficult and uncomfortable challenge to modern expectations (we have become used to viewing characters as partly constructed by the real person of the actor). Ultimately the responses to Hall's *Oresteia* go to show that the challenge of translating ancient costume is both one of the difference of semiotic code, and also of the semiotic process; performances are now operating in their own theatrical environments where traditions, expectations, and ways of viewing have all changed. For further discussion of ancient mask and the issues involved in adopting it in modern theatre, see Vervain and Wiles (2001).

The use of modern costume can, on the other hand, solve some of the problems which we have just seen with the use of authentic costume (though it also imports issues of its own). The major drawback of the mask or overly-authentic costume is its inaccessibility for many viewers and therefore its creation of a sense of alienation. The use of modern costume can resolve this issue and allow the stage action to become more accessible to the audience, which allows it to have a greater impact. Katie Mitchell, one of the most prominent contemporary theatre directors of Greek tragedy, chooses modern costume in her productions for precisely this reason. In an interview about her production of Euripides' *Women of Troy*, staged at the National Theatre, London in 2007, she says (interview by Jane Edwardes, *Time Out*, 12 November 2007):

> There's something about dressing actors in tunics and Jesus sandals, or about an attempt to do a reconstruction with masks which I think distances the viewer from the reality contained in the material. You go 'Thank heavens we don't behave like that now.'

Hattie Morahan, who played Iphigenia in Katie Mitchell's 2004 production of Euripides' *Iphigenia at Aulis* at the National Theatre, London, offers further insight into the thinking behind this directorial choice (interview by Joe Mahon in *Theatregoer*, July 2004):

> We're not in sandals and togas. We're doing the play with a 1940s/1950s look because if you have people in ancient Greek costume it alienates the audience and allows them to distance themselves. We wanted to do it in some

kind of recognisably modern setting, but it can't be too modern because of the social relations of the play. The status of women, for example, wouldn't sit particularly well with anything post-1960 – it'd seem anachronistic.

The difference between the alienating effect of ancient costume and the accessibility of more modern costume, which Morahan refers to here, can be felt immediately by comparing the image of Hall's *Oresteia* (Fig. 21) with an image of Mitchell's *Iphigenia at Aulis* (Fig. 22). Morahan's second point (in this quotation) draws attention to one of the issues of using modern costume: while it has the advantage of making the production accessible to the viewers and enabling them to relate to the action, it brings with it a set of cultural assumptions which might conflict with those of the play. Costume which is iconic for a set period has a whole world embedded in it: the social conditions, political movements, and cultural ideas of a time and place. This cluster of ideas is evoked along with the time setting and imported into the playworld. So costume which suggests a time period after the 1960s, also invites the assumption that the liberal thinking which emerged in that period, forms a part of the playworld. From this point of view, the 1940s/1950s costuming for the *Iphigenia* shows a great sensitivity to one of the issues of translating costume. The choice succeeded in making the action seem relevant, while also retaining the coherence of the play and its ideological assumptions. It also, though it is not clear whether this was a part of the intention, created a time setting strikingly similar to the type of past which we have seen constructed in ancient productions.

Both the Mitchell production and ancient production operate with a playworld set in the past. We have seen one reason, in Morahan's comments, why the past was chosen. But it is striking that Mitchell did not select a specific year for the action of the play. The dating of the costume was rather ambiguous: see the dresses of Clytemnestra and the Chorus in Fig. 22. Among the reviews, some identify the time setting as 1930s/1940s, others firmly 1940s, and others still 1950s. In terms of the meaning created through the relationship between the time period and the content of the play, it actually makes quite a difference whether it is 1930s (pre-war), 1940s (war-time), or 1950s (post-war). Yet Mitchell leaves the time setting rather non-specific and so does not force the parallels or connections; it could be anywhere around those dates. The production is simply set some time in our society's past, around the middle of last century. This, of course, is exactly how the mythological setting operated in fifth-century productions of ancient tragedy. Tragedies were not 'historical' plays as such, but are definitely set in the society's past to offer some distance to the viewers. Nevertheless, the ancient audience could also watch the action through a double vision, relating it to contemporary events at given moments in the play and often at the prompting of some pieces of costume. Similarly for the costuming of the Mitchell production,

Fig. 22. Iphigenia with Clytemnestra and Chorus in Mitchell's
Iphigenia at Aulis.

while the overall look sets it somewhere in the 1940s/1950s, there are some elements which zoom the action into the present. Iphigenia's wedding dress, for example, is not particularly 40s or 50s in style, and in any case as an iconic garment it transcends set time periods (Fig. 22). As a piece of clothing which is familiar from the contemporary world outside the theatre, it invites the audience to view the stage action with a double vision and to make a connection with the present. So while the modern costume in general had the virtue of being accessible, this element, in particular, allowed the impact of the production to be even more direct. On the surface the choice of modern costuming may seem like a kind of rejection of the ancient plays, or their setting, and yet in this example we have seen how through this choice a very similar experience of the play (in terms of the fluidity of the time setting and the double-vision it allows) could be created.

If, on the other hand, the costuming in a modern production is entirely contemporary, then it loses the impact of shifts between past and present that were possible in ancient performances. This kind of production using contemporary dress issues a demand, rather than an invitation, to think of the action in relation to the world outside the theatre. The time setting of the play in this scenario is one-dimensional in the same sense as the use of ancient dress risks being; here the one dimension is the present, there it is the past. But in fifth-century tragedy the dynamic of the action and the power of its impact come in part from the fluid interaction between past and present to which the costume could contribute. The use of entirely contemporary dress, and the directness it lends to the action, perhaps maximises the impact, but operates, as theatre, in a different way from Greek tragedy in its original performance context.

The use of modern costume, if handled sensitively, can help to make the action accessible while still preserving a sense of the type of world within which ancient tragedy operated. It also has the potential to offer solutions to the serious challenge, already mentioned, of finding a semiotic equivalence so that the costume means the same as, or has a similar dramatic effect to, the original. Ancient costume is limited in what it can mean to the modern audience who cannot be expected to be familiar with all the semiotic codes or have a full knowledge of the language of tragic costume. For the costuming strategy of a fifth-century Greek tragedy to be meaningful in a modern production, it is necessary to translate it and find equivalents. The use of modern dress gives a greater scope for this translation process because it offers a whole range of costume pieces which have semiotic significance for the audience. This approach is arguably more 'authentic' (than attempted ancient reconstruction) since the director or costume designer is, like the ancient playwright, working with the signs available in the world of his/her audience. Using modern costume opens up possibilities for finding semiotic equivalents and through this to allow the language of a play's costuming to speak in the way in which it was intended. Modern costume may more readily communicate meaning to the audience since it operates within the framework of a familiar semiotic code. While this is a major advantage to choosing modern costume, there is also necessarily the danger of importing unwanted modern associations and imposing these onto the ancient play through the costuming (see below). Even so, modern costuming undeniably has the advantage over ancient in terms of its potential to provide the means of allowing the audience to understand the meaning and effect of the original costuming strategy.

Finding semiotic equivalents, however, is not always as easy as it sounds and there are some serious challenges to the director in the costuming strategies of ancient plays. How, for example, is it possible to find a modern semiotic equivalent to the death clothing used in Euripides' *Heracles* (among other plays) which signifies a character's imminent death and is sensed to propel him or her towards it? (see Chapter 4). Death clothing is, crucially, *not* the same as mourning wear (which would produce a very different momentum), and therefore dressing the characters in black is not really a meaningful solution. What the character puts on in the ancient tragedies is essentially his/her clothing for the coffin, and so it might be possible to produce this effect by using very formal wear with stiffly coiffured hair or even, for real shock factor which after all Heracles' reaction implies, body-bags ready for the mortuary. It would also be possible to use expensive-looking clothing, as finery, and to allow the text to do the work in constructing the sense of doom surrounding it; but this solves only half of the problem in some cases, since death clothing could also carry the ambiguity of being wedding clothing in ancient Greece and this, too, was exploited on the tragic stage (see Chapter 4). Here is a case where it becomes impossible to find an equivalent since it simply does not exist. While verbally explaining it could set up the symbolism, it would nevertheless be limited in effect since it refers to a custom which is alien to us. In Mitchell's production of Euripides' *Iphigenia* (see above), Iphigenia, who is expecting to marry Achilles (but will be sacrificed by her father instead), appears on stage in a modern iconic white wedding dress (Fig. 22). While this loses some of the force of the original costuming, which would presumably have been ambiguous finery (*kosmos*) and would have pointed ironically both to Iphigenia's wedding and her death, it has other merits as a costume choice. It is still able to create *pathos* by the contrast between the happy occasion which it should signify and the reality of the young woman's situation (of which the audience remains painfully aware). Mitchell sees the potential of the cultural associations with the iconic wedding dress and exploits them to create a dramatic effect similar (though without the same tension of 'determinism', on which see Chapter 4) to the original. The other advantage to the choice of this iconic and culturally-anchored wedding dress is that it encourages the audience to view the action as both past and present (see above).

In the case of the wedding dress, its current symbolic associations worked well within the context of the play, but in other cases costume can import modern associations into the playworld which change the effect of the original. One of the most difficult pieces of cloth in Greek tragedy for which to find a semiotic equivalent is the one spread on the ground before Agamemnon in Aeschylus' *Agamemnon* 931-72. The difficulty is in the semiotic richness of this cloth in this scene. The many layers of symbolic meaning embedded in the cloth make Agamemnon's stage action of walking on it one of the most powerful moments in the play (see Taplin 1978, 79-83). But finding an equivalent is difficult, since cloth is not a symbol of value or stored-up wealth in our society. In Peter Hall's *Oresteia*, a fine red cloth was used and to compensate for the failure of the cloth to suggest wealth inherently (as purple sea-dyed cloth would have in the ancient world), it was laid out so that it looked like a red carpet. This solved one problem in the sense that it conveyed the idea of a self-seeking status gesture (which the cloth alone could not have done), but it imported unhelpful associations too. The red carpet is usually seen in positive terms in our society and symbolises the wealth and status of those who walk on it, but they are intended to tread on the carpet and few begrudge or criticise the gesture. In *Agamemnon* the act is culturally transgressive, risks criticism (from the gods and the people), and spoils wealth in a way which symbolically echoes or replays Agamemnon's actions at Aulis and Troy. The red carpet cannot convey any of this. Katie Mitchell in her production of the *Oresteia* at the National Theatre, London, 1999-2000, took a radically different approach and used a cloth made up of the blood-stained dresses of little girls. This created an emotional impact, not for the same reasons but perhaps on a similar level to the trampling of the cloth in the original production. But again something is lost in translation, since the nature of the stage action changes entirely if the spoiling has already been done – the cloth of dresses represents past actions and while it is an effective symbol of them, when Agamemnon treads on the cloth in Mitchell's production it is not a replay of the spoiling before our eyes. The shock factor in the Mitchell is transferred from the stage action to the cloth. The use of the dresses also privileges one layer of symbolism over all the others (i.e. the killing of Iphigenia) and therefore simplifies the reason for Agamemnon's murder. The beauty of the original sea-purple cloth is the complexity of its symbolism and the ambiguity that this creates around the question of the justice of his death (is it the gods or Clytemnestra acting?). If a modern production really wanted to find an equivalent to the idea of spoiling of wealth which is actually at the core of this stage action, then something like setting alight to a trail of bank notes might convey the shocking recklessness of the act (and Agamemnon's reluctance to do it), but again it would only manage to translate one aspect of the cloth's symbolism. This example shows just how difficult it can be to find semiotic equivalents and to reconstruct the multivalence of the original costuming strategy; translations necessarily involve a process of selection in terms of the meaning which will be privileged in the costuming of a modern production.

The example of the 'red carpet' points to the difficulty there can be in the associations surrounding a semiotic entity in our culture. In that case, the symbol and its associations were evoked deliberately in order to try to offer the audience some way of understanding the significance of the sea-purple cloth in the original play; it was a choice by Hall rather than one demanded by the prop in the text. In other cases the play text requires the representation on stage of a piece of costume which now carries different associations. If the production is in modern dress, then the costume will import these associations and the director has to mediate this in some way.

One of the most striking examples of costume in Greek tragedy which now carries a radically different set of associations is the veil (or the action of veiling the head with the *himation*). On the ancient Greek stage the veil could be used to symbolise modesty or shame or retreat from the world (e.g. Phaedra in Euripides' *Hippolytus* 243-6, Heracles in Euripides' *Heracles* 1159f., and Niobe in Aeschylus' *Niobe* (see Chapter 4); see Cairns 1996). But for a modern audience, the veil is now closely associated with heated political debate over religious issues. There is no cancelling out of this symbolism, especially since the veil is no longer otherwise part of everyday wear (as it was in ancient Greece). A veil in modern society is the symbol of a religious statement and ideological position. This presents the director with a challenge, since while the equivalent (in material terms) garment to the ancient one exists in our society, it carries inescapable semiotic associations. One of the most effective solutions to this is to exploit this unavoidable association. This was done, for example, in *Lisa's Sex Strike*, Blake Morrison's adaptation of Aristophanes' *Lysistrata*, produced in 2007, where the spat about the veil (lines 530-4 in the original) was made intensely topical. This costuming choice introduced a religious dimension to the gender argument which was not in the original, and some could say that it made Aristophanes say something he never wanted to say. And yet the dramatic impact and shock factor of this moment in the production could be argued to reconstruct something of the original effect. The challenge to the modern director is to recognise the shift in cultural associations around certain pieces of costume and then to find a way of working with this (through either exploiting it or side-stepping it). For further discussion of the issues surrounding costume in modern productions of ancient drama, see Llewellyn-Jones (2001).

The choice between whether to do a production in ancient or modern costume comes down to a question of priorities. Both have advantages and disadvantages, and demand the privileging of one consideration over another. Ancient costume, whether notionally 'authentic' or actually historically accurate, distances the audience and puts some limit on the possibility of reproducing all the effects of the costume and its manipulation in the original. Alternatively, modern costume can have the potential to produce a much closer translation, in terms of impact, of the fifth-century costuming strategy, but necessarily puts the action directly into a contemporary, or near contemporary, context. In the end, it is the subjective viewpoint of what is important to a production of tragedy which makes the choice between the two. Bieber, for example, in her brief assessment of costuming options and their merits, dismisses the use of modern dress in productions of Greek tragedy (see Bieber 1961, 268-9). But the question of semiotics and the creation of meaning does not come into her assessment criteria, far more important for her was the reconstruction of the 'true spirit' of the Greeks. The historical context of a production, and society's attitude to the ancient Greeks at the time of a performance, play into the choices that are made for costume and influence the view of priorities. While at the present, the most important consideration for a production might be dramatic impact and the effective communication of message, at other periods in the performance history of tragedy authenticity has been the order of the day. This range in approaches can offer a spectrum of interpretations of any given tragedy, and while no production could recreate the exact fifth-century impact of the costume, each version has the potential to bring out some aspect of it or even to create new meanings from it. In this sense, the challenge of costuming tragedy in fact becomes a highly creative and productive process from which it is possible to learn more about tragedy and the theatrical experience it is capable of constructing. For a fuller discussion of the theoretical issues surrounding the translation of the costuming strategies of fifth-century tragedy, see Wyles (2010a).

Conclusion

Each of the three great tragedians of fifth-century Athens is remembered within antiquity for something to do with costume. Aeschylus apparently brought in the sleeves, the trailing robes, painted masks, and high boots, Sophocles introduced white boots, and Euripides dressed his characters in rags! (see Chapter 5 for rags, and the Appendix). But in terms of the contribution made by each to the semiotics of costume and its language as it developed in fifth-century tragedy, these traditions miss the point. If we step beyond costume as a material entity, then the tragedian who apparently brought the level of costuming down, Euripides, in fact had the most to contribute by the creativity and sophistication of the use of costume in his plays. It may be slightly unfair to judge the three in this way when so many more of Euripides' plays survive (providing more material to judge from), but the overall impression in his tragedies is of a confident and sophisticated use of costume. This is only made possible through the groundwork of Aeschylus, who, as we have seen, was very interested in engaging with the ideas surrounding the semiotic process of reading costume and was also capable of exploiting costume to the maximum in his plays.

Aeschylus' contribution to tragic costume was not, as the ancient sources suggest, in adding to its grandeur, but in laying out some of the fundamental rules for how to manipulate it in order to create dramatic meaning or a comment on theatre. His plays and the iconic use of costume in them would also offer Euripides material to ghost/recycle; so that in this sense, it is Aeschylus who allows Euripides to be so creative with costume. How ironic that Euripides' apparent adversary in the *Frogs*, who criticises his use of costume, should in fact prove to be the basis for it.

Sophocles' contribution is more of a challenge to determine. The impression of his general interest in costume and his techniques for handling it shifts depending on where we look; so, for example, while in his *Philoctetes* he makes one element of costume (the bow) the pivotal focus of the action, in his *Antigone* there are very few references to costume. This case warns against generalising too quickly about any of the tragedians' characteristic approaches to costume, since so many plays have been lost. Since costuming strategies were not 'dictated' by what had gone before, it is, perhaps, more helpful to think of each play as a fresh opportunity for a playwright to experiment with costume and to contribute to its language.

Costume and its use in the tragedies must be understood in a context.

127

Not just in the historical or cultural context of fifth-century Athens, but in its theatrical context. Important considerations for this are the special conditions of the festival, with its continuity of audience and its tendency towards spending (both of which have implications for the semiotics of costume), and the performance history that was created there. Each production is not set out on a blank canvas but is performed on a stage full of the memories and ghosts of previous plays. The past experience brings expectations about costume and also potentially adds to the layers of its meaning in the play being performed. Any use of costume in tragedy is categorised and understood in relation to this performance history and may make its own contribution to it. The language of costume develops in this way through the use, reuse, and innovation in the costuming of each play. At the same time, there is a theatrical discourse, expressed through costume, running through this performance history which even occasionally generates meaning through reference to the comic handling of costume. Looking at costume from this perspective can open up other layers to its meaning within a play and also reveal the playwright's theoretical thinking on costume and theatre in general. Understanding this has implications beyond an appreciation of ancient Greek tragedy, since ancient drama offers the foundations not only to the play texts in the Western tradition but also to their use of semiotics.

Even without being able to recreate this specific performance context, seeing tragedy in performance can bring out many of the costuming effects which can otherwise be missed when looking at a printed text. Modern productions can enable the force of the original costuming strategy to be brought back to life. So, for example, Mitchell's use of a wedding dress for Iphigenia (see Chapter 6), allowed the impact and dramatic effectiveness of that costuming choice by Euripides to be felt in a fresh and direct way. Modern performances cannot tell us everything, as a part of the meaning or effect is inevitably lost in translation (the wedding dress does not have the same ambiguity as ancient bridal/death clothing). But they nevertheless provide excellent thinking material, especially for trying to understand the dynamic created through costume. Also, considering the challenges of costuming in a modern production draws attention to the theoretical issues surrounding translating costume across cultures. This can be especially helpful for the case of tragic costume in Rome, where elements of continuity can obscure the differences in meaning created by this new cultural context. The response of modern directors to the costume strategies of the ancient playwrights can also bring out unexpected meanings in the play which invite a reassessment of our interpretation of it. So while a knowledge of tragic costume may enhance our appreciation of theatre today (since it is the basis of it), at the same time modern productions of tragedy may help us to a better understanding of the costuming strategies of the tragedians.

The plays themselves, though, are of course the first place to start, and a re-examination of the texts with eyes wide-open to costuming can invite a reassessment of our understanding of the plays or tragedy more generally. Even the simplest first analysis of costume, a list of where it is referred to in the surviving tragedies (see the List of References to Costume in Tragedies), can be revealing. First, the number of plays where a character is wearing a garland or wreath points to the wide usage of an easily missed 'alien' visual element of the tragic world. Clearly for the ancient audience, who probably wore garlands themselves when watching the performances (see Chapter 4), the sight would not seem an odd one. But for a modern audience, this commonplace visual element of the tragic world is potentially to some extent as alienating as the use of masks (see Chapter 6). Every time the garland or wreath is mentioned it draws attention to what could be an alienating piece of costume (rather than, as the costuming strategy originally intended, reinforcing whatever symbolic meaning it has within the play). Secondly, the general rule of keeping murder or suicide off-stage in Greek tragedy can lead to the impression that this drama was not violent. But the number of references to swords (often drawn) in the plays suggests that the audience must have sensed the latent potential for violence in many tragedies. Even if they 'knew' that violence was unlikely to take place on stage, the references to the swords and drawing them must, nevertheless, have created tension. These are just two examples of where costume can invite us to rethink tragedy. In a more specific way, looking at the references for any given play gives an immediate sense of whether an element of costume dominates its semiotic field and becomes the symbolic focus of the action. This in its turn gives an indication of which elements of costume were likely to have become iconically associated with the play after its performance.

The initial impressions that the list can offer are striking, even if there are admittedly some limitations to what it can tell us when so many tragedies are now lost (restricting our view of the picture). Further insights, however, come from following the references in the list and analysing them in the context of their plays, in relation to other plays, and in terms of the language of costume set out in Chapters 3 and 4. There was no way of discussing every single reference to costume in this book, yet each one has a different story to tell about dramatic technique, meaning in the play, and even theatre more generally. It is my hope that this book will inspire readers to explore for themselves the costuming in more of the plays, and through this come to appreciate the brilliance of costume in Greek tragedy.

Appendix

The written sources for costume in the fifth century BC are late, unreliable, and problematic. As pieces of evidence they tell us more about costume, or attitudes towards it, in the period that they were written, than in tragedy's original performance context. I include a selection here, nevertheless, to make clear the basis for many of the ideas about costume (both within antiquity and in modern discussions).

(1) *Life of Aeschylus* 2 and 14. Probably late Hellenistic. Greek text available in *TGrF* 3, Test. A1, pp. 31-7. Translation here based on Csapo and Slater (1994, 4.2, p. 260).

> **2** <Aeschylus> began making tragedies when young and he greatly surpassed his predecessors in poetry, in the arrangement of the *skene*, and in the brilliance of the furnishings and the costumes of the actors and the grandeur of the chorus, as Aristophanes also attests (*Frogs* 1004f.): 'O first of the Greeks to fortify grandiose speech and adorn tragic blather ...'

> **14** Aeschylus first increased tragedy's stature by presenting the noblest sufferings and he adorned his stage and dazzled the gaze of his audience with splendour, paintings, and devices, altars and graves, trumpet blasts, apparitions, Furies, covering his actors with sleeves and long trains (*syrma*), giving the mask the *onkos*, and raising them aloft with larger buskins (*kothornoi*)

(2) *Suda* lexicon *ai* 357 (Adler). Written at end of the tenth century AD. The translation is my own.

> This man [Aeschylus] was the first to invent the practice of tragic actors using masks painted marvellously with colours and wearing shoes (*arbulai*) known as *embatai*.

(3) *Life of Sophocles* 6. Probably late Hellenistic. According to this biography, Istros (a scholar active in the mid-third century BC) had claimed that Sophocles was involved in the development of tragic footwear. Greek text available in *TGrF* 3, Test. A1, pp. 31-7, or Pickard-Cambridge (1968, 205). The translation is my own.

> Istros says that he [Sophocles] invented the white boots (*crepides*) that actors and chorusmen wear.

(4) Horace, *On the Art of Poetry* 275-80. Translation Rudd (1997).

We are told Thespis discovered the genre of the tragic Muse which was never known before; he carried his plays on a wagon to be sung and acted by men who had smeared lees on their faces. After him came Aeschylus, introducing the mask and lordly robe; he laid a stage on lowish supports and called for a sonorous diction and the wearing of high-soled boots.

(5) Philostratus, *Life of Apollonius Tyana* 6.11. Written in the early third century AD. Translation Conybeare (1912), slightly modified.

On the one hand as a poet, he [Aeschylus] set himself to make his diction worthy of tragedy, on the other hand as a manager, to adapt his stage to sublime, rather than humble and grovelling, themes. Accordingly he devised masks which represented the forms of the heroes, and he mounted his actors on buskins so that their gait might correspond to the characters they played; and he was the first to devise costumes, which might convey an adequate impression to the audience of the heroes and heroines they saw.

(6) Philostratus, *Life of the Sophists* 1.9.1. Written between 217 and 238 AD. Translation Wright (1989), slightly modified.

Sicily produced Gorgias of Leontini, and we must consider that the art of the sophists carries back to him as though he were its father. For if we reflect how many additions Aeschylus made to tragedy when he furnished her with her proper costume and the high-soled buskins, with the types of heroes, with messengers who tell what has happened at home and abroad, and with the conventions as to what must be done on the stage and in front of it, then we find that this is what Gorgias in his turn did for his fellow-craftsmen.

(7) Themistius, *Oration* 26.316d. Mid-fourth century AD. Translation Penella (2000).

Did stately tragic drama enter the theatre fully equipped at once with chorus and actors? Do we not pay heed to Aristotle? He tells us that first the chorus came forth and sang to the gods, then Thespis introduced the prologue and the spoken lines, thirdly Aeschylus introduced <two> actors and the buskins and the further refinements of tragedy that we enjoyed were the work of Sophocles and Euripides.

(8) Cramer, *Anecdota Parisiensia* 1.19 (recorded on a manuscript held in the Royal Library, Paris). Translation here based on Csapo and Slater (1994, 4.56, p. 261).

If someone wishes to attribute to Aeschylus all the inventions of the stage – *ekkyklemata* ('rollers-out'), *periaktoi* ('revolvers-about'), *mechanai* ('machines'), *exostra* ('out-shovers'), *proscenia*, *distegia* ('second stories'), lightning observatories, thunder machines, *theologeia* ('places where the gods talk'), and *geranoi* ('cranes'), and of course also the *xystides*, *batrachides* (frog-green garments), masks and buskins, and those *poikila* (elaborate tragic robes), *syrmata* ('trailing tragic robes'), the *kalyptra* ('veils'), *kolpoma* ('overgarment with ample folds'), *parapechu* ('woman's garment with purple border on each side') and *agrenon* ('woollen netlike shawl'), and the third actor added to the second – or if Sophocles also devised and invented some of these things; those who wish can argue about this and drag the credit in either direction.

(9) Pollux, *Onomasticon* 4.115-20 and 133-42. Pollux lived in the second century AD and recorded stage antiquities in Book 4 of his *Onomasticon*. The evidence he offers for tragic costume is tantalising, since it is one of the only substantial descriptions of costume from antiquity, but the difficulty with it is that it is in a fragmentary state (which already limits the clarity of its meaning) and it is not even sure which period of performance history Pollux is discussing in his work (see Pickard-Cambridge 1968, 177-9). Translation from Csapo and Slater (1994, 395-400, with some modification).

4.115f. On tragic costume:

> ... footwear in tragedy are buskins (*kothornoi*) and *embades* ('step-ins'); while *embatai* are comic. Tragic clothes are the *poikilon* ('embroidered') – so the *chiton* was called – and the overgarments are the *xystis*, *batrachis* ('frog-coloured'), *chlanis*, gilded *chlamys*, gilt-edged, the *statos*, *phoinikis* ('scarlet cloak'), <and tragic headgear are the> *tiara*, *kalyptra* (veil), *mitra*. The *agrenon* was a woven woollen netlike shawl that covered the body, which Teiresias put on or some other soothsayer. The *kolpoma* was what Atreuses or Agamemnons or that sort put on over their *poikila*; the *ephaptis* was a sort of red or scarlet binding that warriors or hunters wore on their hand. The *krokotos* ('crocus dress', i.e. saffron-coloured) is a *himation* (i.e. overdress). Dionysus used it and a flowery *maschalister* (breast-strap?) and a thyrsus. Those in distress wore dirty white clothes, especially fugitives, or grey or black or yellowish or bluish grey. Philoktetes and Telephus are dressed in rags. Also fawn skins, leather jackets, cutlasses, sceptres, spears, bows, quivers, messengers' staffs, clubs, lion skins, and suits of armour are all part of tragic male costume. Female is the purple *syrtos* (dress with a train), the white *parapechy* (a garment which covers the forearms and has a purple border on each side) of the queen. The *syrtos* of a woman in distress is black, the throwover blue grey or yellowish.

4.133-42 Tragic and satyr masks:

> Now these would be the tragic masks: shaven man, white, greying, black, blond, blondish. (OLD MEN.) These are old men: (1) The shaven man is the oldest, with white hair; the hair is attached to the *onkos*. The *onkos* is the bit above the face of the mask rising to a peak. The shaven man has a clean-shaven chin. (2) The white man's hair is entirely gray, and he has curls around the head, a firm chin, and jutting eyebrows and off-white complexion. The *onkos* is short. (3) The graying (?) man represents people who are

naturally going white, and he is black and sallow. (4) The name of the black man comes from his complexion, and he is curly around the chin and head; the face is rough, and the *onkos* big. (5) The blond man has blond curls and a smaller *onkos* and has a good complexion. (6) The blondish man is otherwise similar save that he is smaller and represents sick characters.

(YOUNG MEN.) The masks of young men are the excellent, the curly, the partly curly, the delicate, the squalid, the second squalid, yellowish, the partly yellowish. (7) The excellent is viewed as oldest of the young men, beardless, well-complexioned, but getting dark (around the chin); his hair is thick and black. (8) The curly is blond with an excessive *onkos*. The hair is attached to the *onkos*. His eyebrows are raised, his appearance vigorous. (9) The partly curly, in other respects like the previous, is younger. (10) The delicate is blond with ringlets, white-complexioned, cheery, a model of a handsome god. (11) The squalid has a large *onkos*, is somewhat livid, downcast, grubby, with long blond hair. (12) The second squalid is as much thinner than the previous one as he is younger. (13) The yellowish has puffy flesh and lots of hair, slightly blond with a sickly complexion, such as suits a ghost or a wounded man. (14) The partly yellowish is in other respects like the excellent but is yellowish to denote sickness or love.

(SLAVES.) The masks of the servants are the goatskin wearer, spade-beard, *anasillos* (= with Persian haircut). (15) The goatskin wearer has no *onkos*, but has a cap and long, combed-out white hair, and a yellowish, whitish face, a harsh nose, high forehead, and glowering eyes. He is yellowish, with a prominent jaw. (16) The spade-beard is in his prime and has a high broad *onkos*, with a furrow around the periphery <of his *onkos*>. He is blond, rough, ruddy-complexioned, suitable for a messenger. (17) The *anasillos* is blond with an excessive *onkos*. His hair is drawn back from the centre; he has no beard and is slightly ruddy. He too is a messenger.

(WOMEN.) The masks of women are the gray long-haired, the old free woman, the old servant woman, the old woman shaven in the middle, the woman in the goatskin, the long-haired yellow woman, the shaven-in-the-middle yellow, the shaven-in-the-middle fresh, the shorn girl, the second shorn girl, the maiden. (18) The grey long-haired is greater in age and prestige than the rest, white-haired with moderate *onkos*, sallow. In old times she was called partly yellow. (19) The old free woman is rather golden in complexion with a small *onkos*. Her hair comes down to her shoulders; she hints at misfortune. (20) The old servant woman has a cap of lambskin instead of an *onkos*, and has a wrinkled skin. (21) The old servant woman shaven in the middle has a short *onkos*, white skin, partly yellow complexion, and is not altogether gray. (22) The woman in the goatskin is younger than her and has no *onkos*. (23) The long-haired yellow woman has black hair, a disagreeable look, and her complexion is as her name suggests. (24) The shaven-in-the-middle yellow woman is like the long-haired one, except for one bit shaven from the middle. (25) The fresh shaven-in-the-middle woman has her hair cut like the one before, but no longer the yellowness. (26) The shorn girl has instead of an *onkos* a parting in her brushed-down hair, and it is cut short all round; her complexion is sallow. (27) The second shorn girl is like the first except for the parting and the curls all around, as if she had been long in distress. (28) The maiden is a young mask, like Danae or another young girl.

The supplementary masks: Actaeon horned, or Phineus blind; Thamyris with one eye blue and the other black; Argos with many eyes; Euhippe daughter of Cheiron changing into a horse in Euripides, or Tyro, with livid cheeks in Sophocles – she has got this from being beaten by her mother-in-law Sidero-; Achilles shorn in mourning for Patroclus; Amymone; or a river or a mountain; Gorgon or Justice, Death, Fury, Rage, Madness, Hybris, Centaur, Titan, Giant, Indus, Triton, perhaps also Polis, Priam (?), Persuasion, Muses, Hours, Nymphs of Mikathos (?), Pleiades, Illusion, Drunkenness, Dread, and Envy. Well, while these could also be comic, satyric masks are grey-haired satyr, bearded satyr, beardless satyr, grandfather Silenus (= Papposilenus). The masks are alike in all respects, except for the variations indicated by their names, e.g., the Papposilenus is more bestial in appearance.

Glossary

This glossary is selective and offers definitions of the terms mentioned in the discussion or relevant to tragedy. For any clothing terms not listed here, see Cleland et al. (2007). All Greek and Latin terms are italicised.

aegis: Athena's equivalent to a breastplate, it hangs like a short rounded poncho over her shoulders and is normally patterned with scales, the Gorgon's head, and serpent fringing.

anaxyrides: trousers, associated with 'barbarian' (foreign) figures (see Figs 2 and 6).

arbulai: shoes. This is the standard term used by characters in tragedy to refer to shoes.

caduceus: wand, typically carried by Hermes, representing his role as messenger of the gods and leader of the dead to the underworld, often decorated with two serpents twisted round it and wings at the top.

chiton: basic robe, made by pinning a rectangle of woven cloth around the body. It could be pinned in Ionic style (see Fig. 17), or Doric (see Fig. 18).

chlamys: a short wool cloak worn by males.

corslet: breastplate (see Fig. 10).

cothurni: Latin name for the high-soled stage boots used by tragic actors in the Roman period. Despite the misleading claims by Roman writers that these stage boots were used in fifth-century Greece, the Greek term *kothornoi* does not refer to this type of boot (see below) and there seems to have been more freedom in tragic footwear at this early stage.

crepides: high boots.

diadem: headband which could be plain or patterned (see Fig. 5).

diphthera: the Greek term simply means 'prepared hide' or piece of leather, so it may be used to refer to any garment made out of leather.

embatai: half boots, made of felt.

eumarides: slippers associated with 'barbarian' (foreign) figures.

fawnskin: see *nebris*.

fillet: often used to translate the Greek term *tainia*, which was a ribbon or decorative band. It could be used to tie the hair or religiously, to adorn a suppliant branch, or tomb (see Fig. 1, tomb on left).

'girdle': often used as the translation of the Greek term (*zone*), which was simply the belt tied round the waist to gather in a robe. A better English translation might be sash. (See Figs 7 and 9a.)

137

greaves: shin guards, worn as part of armour for battle. Heracles is shown wearing an elaborately patterned pair on the Pronomos vase (Fig. 9b).

himation: thick cloak, made up simply from a rectangle of woven cloth, wrapped round.

kalyptra: a woman's veil. This is a separate garment, though often when characters veil their heads in tragedy, they may simply use their clothing to do it.

kandys: shaped like a cardigan, this garment could be worn off the shoulders (without arms in its sleeves). Associated with 'barbarian' (foreign) figures.

kidaris: floppy hat with flaps, associated with 'barbarian' (foreign) figures (see Figs 2a and 6).

kothornoi (see *cothurni*): high boot later associated with tragic perform- ances, but in the fifth century used to refer to a boot that could be pulled onto either foot and was associated with women (see Fig. 5).

nebris: the skin of a fawn (young deer) often described as 'dappled' (with white spots). Often worn, tied around the upper body, by maenads/ bacchants, followers of Dionysus (see Fig. 4).

onkos: the raised hair-do/high headpiece that had become a standard part of tragic masks by the Roman period (see Figs 14 and 15).

pallium: the Latin term for the Greek *himation* (cloak).

peplos: basic word used for male and female clothing in tragedy. The term refers to the basic rectangle of woven cloth which could be pinned to make up a garment (see *chiton*), used as a cloak, or as blankets, wall coverings etc. *Peplos* can be used in all these senses in tragedy.

phallus: an exaggerated costume penis, made in leather and used on the comic stage (see Fig. 11).

pilos: conical felt hat (see Aegisthus in Fig. 11).

sakkos: often translated as 'snood', this 'tea-cosy' hat covered most of the hair (see Fig. 4).

skeue: term meaning 'kit' or 'equipment' in Greek and used to refer to stage costume (including props and masks).

snood, see *sakkos*.

stephane: headdress (see Figs 1 and 7).

thyrsus: a stick (fennel stalk) decorated with ivy and vine-leaves, carried by the followers of Dionysus (maenads/bacchants).

tiara: pointed decorative hat associated with 'barbarian' (foreign) figures (see Fig. 9 (on the mask held by the woman at the end of the couch) and Fig. 19).

toga: archetypal Roman garment, made by draping a piece of cloth around the body.

List of References to Costume in Tragedies

I offer here a list of references made to costume in surviving tragedy. I have excluded fragmentary plays; for those references see Dingel (1967). By costume, I mean the clothing or accessories worn by the characters or which have the potential to be worn by characters in the plays (so, for example, I include the armour brought on stage in Aeschylus' *Seven against Thebes*). Some of the references are made directly about the costumes while they are on stage, while others are comments made about them before they are visible or after they have gone from stage; I consider both categories useful for the analysis of the symbolism developed for a costume. I have excluded the references to clothing which do not relate to the costumes in the play (so, for example, the chorus' mention of Hera's shoe in Euripides' *Heracles* 1304, is not listed here). While these 'unrelated' references give a general impression of the type of clothing understood to exist in the tragic world, they are not directly linked to the costuming strategy. The list is as complete as possible, although there may be some references which I have missed; ultimately it is intended only as a starting point for looking at costuming and is no substitute for the close reading or re-reading of the plays themselves.

aegis: A. *Eum.* 404
armour: A. *Supp.* 182, 839-41; A. *Sept.* 675-6; E. *Heracleidae* 698f., 720-8; E. *IA* 1359; E. *Phoe.* 168, 779; E. *Bacch.* 809; [E.] *Rhes.* 3, 22, 90, 305-6, 382
Bacchic gear (various): E. *Bacch.* 24, 25, 34, 106, 111, 176-7, 180, 205, 240, 249, 251, 253-4, 313, 323, 341, 363, 495-6, 554-5, 696-7, 702-4, 733, 762, 835, 915, 1054-6, 1099, 1156-8, 1386
black clothing/mourning: A. *Cho.* 10-12; A. *Eum.* 352 (implied), 370; A. *Pers.* 607-10 (implied); E. *Alc.* 215-17, 426-7, 751, 923-5; E. *Supp.* 97 (implied); E. *Phoe.* 324-6, 372; E. *Hel.* 1087-8, 1186-7; E. *Or.* 457
bow: A. *Eum.* 181-2; S. *Phil.* (throughout); S. *Trach.* 512; E. *Alc.* 35-40; E. *HF* 460-75, 1377-1385; E. *Hel.* 76; E. *Ion* 108, 158, 173; E. *Or.* 268-74
bracelet: E. *Ion* 1007-9
bridal clothing, see **death clothing**
broom: E. *Ion* 80, 103, 112-14, 145
cloak: A. *Eum.* 1028-9; S. *Ajax* 915f.; E. *Heracleidae* 604; E. *Supp.* 111; E. *HF* 1159; E. *Ion* 967; E. *IT* 312, 1207, 1218; E. *Hec.* 342-4; E. *Hipp.* 606; E. *Or.* 1457; **pinned**: E. *HF* 959; E. *El.* 820; [E.] *Rh.* 442

clothing: clinging to: E. *Alc.* 189; E. *Hec.* 342-4; E. *Tro.* 750; E. *Hipp.*
606; E. *HF* 124-5, 520-1, 627, 629-30, 1399; E. *Heracleidae* 48-9; E. *Hel.*
567, 1629; E. *IA* 1460; **hiding something in**: E. *Hec.* 342-4, 1013, 1161;
E. *Ion* 1033; E. *Hel.* 1574; E. *Or.* 1125, 1457; **tearing**: A. *Pers.* 199, 468,
1060; A. *Cho.* 28-30; A. *Supp.* 120-1, 131-2, 904; **wet with tears**: A.
Cho. 81; E. *Supp.* 978-9; E. *El.* 501-2; **other**: A. *Cho.* 30; E. *HF* 52, 1399;
E. *IT* 312, E. *IA* 951

club: S. *Trach.* 512; E. *HF* 470-1, 991-4

death clothing/bridal wear (*kosmos*): E. *Alc.* 149, 160-1; E. *Med.* 951-4,
980-1; E. *HF* 329, 333-5, 442-3, 525-6, 548-9, 702-3; E. *Supp.* 1054-7; E.
Tro. 1218-20; E. *Hel.* 1279; E. *Bacch.* 857

dress: A. *Sept.* 1039; E. *Phoe.* 1491; E. *Bacch.* 828, 830, 833, 836, 857,
935-8, 1156

dress pins: S. *OT* 1268-9; S. *Trach.* 924-5; E. *Hec.* 923 (implied), 1170-1;
E. *El.* 317-18; E. *Andr.* 832-3 (implied)

fawnskin (*nebris*): E. *Bacch.* 24, 111, 176, 180 (implied), 249, 696-7, 835

finery (not bridal/death): A. *Pers.* 608, 833-4, 849; A. *Ag.* 1271; E. *Alc.*
1050; E. *Heracleidae* 725; E. *El.* 966, 1139-40; E. *Tro.* 451-2, 1022-5; E.
Or. 348-51; E. *Andr.* 147-8; E. *Ion* 326-7

foreign clothing (ethnicity): A. *Pers.* 664; A. *Supp.* 237, 278-83 (masks?),
496; A. *Cho.* 560, 674 (implied); E. *Heracleidae* 725; E. *Hec.* 734-5,
1153-5; E. *El.* 317-18; E. *Tro.* 991-2; E. *Or.* 1370; [E.] *Rh.* 313

garland/wreath: A. *Ag.* 493-4, 1265; A. *Cho.* 1034-5; S. *OT* 82-3, 912-13;
S. *Trach.* 178-9; E. *Alc.* 759, 831-2, 1015; E. *Heracleidae* 71, 124; E.
Hipp. 806-7; E. *Supp.* 359-60; E. *HF* 526, 562; E. *El.* 494-8, 854,
874,882, 887-8; E. *Tro.* 353, 451-2; E. *Ion* 522; E. *Phoe.* 856-8; E. *IA* 436,
756-61, 905, 1080, 1476-7, 1512-13, 1567; E. *Bacch.* 177, 205, 253-4,
313, 323, 341-2, 702-3

girdle/sash: A. *Supp.* 455-67; S. *El.* 452; S. *Ant.* 1222 (implied); E. *Bacch.*
935

Greek clothing: S. *Phil.* 223-4; E. *Heracleidae* 130-1; E. *Andr.* 147-53; E.
IT 246 (implied); E. *Or.* 1470

hair: colour: A. *Pers.* 1056-7, 1063; S. *Ant.* 1093; E. *Med.* 1141; E. *Hipp.*
220, 1343; E. *El.* 515, 1071; E. *HF* 233, 362, 993; E. *Or.* 1532; E. *IA* 175,
681, 756-61, 1366; E. *IT* 173; E. *Phoe.* 308f.; E. *Bacch.* 185, 235, 258;
cropped: E. *Alc.* 215-17, 512; E. *Supp.* 97; E. *El.* 107-8, 148-9, 241, 335;
E. *Hel.* 1087, 1187-8, 1224; E. *Phoe.* 322-3, 372; E. *Or.* 128-9, 457-8; **as
offering**: A. *Cho.* 6-7, 168-80, 226-7; S. *El.* 53, 451; S. *Ajax* 1171-81; E.
Alc. 76; E. *El.* 515-46; **supplication by**: E. *Med.* 709; E. *Supp.* 277,
1099; E. *Andr.* 574; E. *IA* 909; **other**: A. *Pers.* 1062; S. *OC* 1260-1; S.
Ajax 1207-10; E. *El.* 184; E. *Hipp.* 202; E. *HF* 934; E. *Phoe.* 63; E. *Ion*
1266-7; E. *Or.* 223-6, 387; E. *Bacch.* 241, 455, 493, 928-32, 1186-7

hair decoration: E. *Andr.* 147 (*stephane*); E. *Phoen.* 1490-1; E. *Med.* 786,
978-84, 1065-6, 1156f.; E. *Bacch.* 833, 929, 1114-21 (headband)

hat: S. *OC* 313-14 (Thessalian)

horns: [A.] *PV* 674
letter/written tablets: S. *Trach.* 46-8, 156-8; E. *Phoe.* 838; E. *Hipp.* 856f.;
 E. *IA* 304-13; E. *IT* 582-90, 594, 636, 727-94
linen garments: made of *bussos*: A. *Sept.* 1039; E. *Bacch.* 821-2; **made
 of** *sindon*: A. *Supp.* 120-1, 131-2; S. *Ant.* 1222 (noose)
lion skin: E. *HF* 465-6
loosened clothing: E. *Phoe.* 1491; E. *Andr.* 832-3
poisoned robe: S. *Trach.* 580, 602, 612-13, 674, 758, 764, 768-9, 774; E.
 Med. 786-7, 951-9, 978-84, 1065-6,1156f.
purple/red: A. *Ag.* 931f.; A. *Eum.* 1028-9; E. *Or.* 1457 (purple bordered)
quiver: A. *Pers.* 1020
rags/poor clothing: A. *Pers.* 835-6, 847-8, 1018, 1030; S. *El.* 191; S. *Phil.*
 38-9, 274, 309; S. *Trach.* 1103; S. *OC* 555-6, 1258-60, 1597; E. *El.* 185,
 239, 501; E. *Hel.* 415-17, 420f., 554, 1079 (bits of ship); E. *Phoe.* 325
religious wear: **prophetess**: A. *Ag.* 1264-72; E. *Tro.* 256-8, 451-2;
 priestess: E. *IT* 798-9; **temple attendant**: E. *Ion* 327, 522
saffron: **dress**: E. *Phoe.* 1491; **slippers**: A. *Pers.* 661
sandal: Eur. *Or.* 1467-8 (golden)
sceptre/stick/staff: A. *Ag.* 74-5, 1265; A. *Supp.* 247-8; S. *OC* 1354; S. *OT*
 456; S. *El.* 419-21; E. *Andr.* 588; E. *El.* 321; E. *Phoe.* 1539, 1719; E. *IA*
 311, 412, 1194-5
shield: A. *Sept.* 375f.; S. *Ajax* 574-6; E. *Tro.* 1136-42, 1192-9
shoes (*arbulai*): A. *Ag.* 944; E. *Bacch.* 638, 1134; E. *Hipp.* 1189; E. *Or.* 140,
 1470; **without shoes**: [A.] *PV* 135; S. *OC* 349; E. *Ion* 220; see also
 sandal and **slipper**
shroud: A. *Ag.* 1115-26, 1382-3, 1492, 1580; A. *Cho.* 492-4, 557, 985-1015;
 A. *Eum.* 460, 633-4; S. *El.* 1468-74; S. *Ajax* 915f.; E. *El.* 1227-32; E. *Tro.*
 1218-20; E. *Hec.* 611-18
slipper (Persian, *eumaris*): A. *Pers.* 664; E. *Or.* 1370
spear: A. *Supp.* 182, 839-41; E. *Heracleidae* 723-8; E. *Hec.* 1155-6; [E.] *Rh.*
 576
stick/staff, see **sceptre**
suppliant branch: A. *Supp.* 21-2, 159, 191-3, 241, 333-4, 480-1, 506-7; A.
 Cho. 1034-5; A. *Eum.* 40-5; S. *OT* 3, 142-3; E. *Supp.* 10, 102, 259, 265
sword: A. *Ag.* 1651-2; A. *Cho.* 1011; A. *Eum.* 40-5; S. *Ant.* 1231-7, 1308-9;
 S. *Phil.* 1254-6; S. *Ajax* 95, 658, 815, 828, 834, 899, 907, 1032-5; E. *Alc.*
 74-6; E. *Andr.* 547; E. *El.* 225; E. *Phoe.* 267, 276, 363, 593-6, 600,625,
 1677; E. *IA* 970; E. *Hel.* 983, 1574; E. *Bacch.* 634-5; E. *Ion* 1257-8; E.
 Or. 1125, 1457-9, 1470, 1504-26, 1531, 1575, 1608, 1627, 1653; E. *IT*
 296, 322-3, 331-3; [E.] *Rh.* 668-9
thyrsus: E. *Bacch.* 25, 176, 180 (implied), 240, 251, 253-4, 363, 495-6,
 554-5, 704, 733, 762, 835, 941-2, 1054-6, 1099, 1157, 1386
tiara: A. *Pers.* 661
urn/libation vessel : A. *Cho.* 99; S. *El.* 54, 1113-70, 1123-5; E. *Supp.*
 1126, 1159

veils/(un)veiling: A. *Supp.* 120-1, 131-2; S. *El.* 1468-70; S. *Ajax* 245-6, 915-16, 1003; S. *Trach.* 1078; E. *Alc.* 1121-2; E. *Heracleidae* 604; E. *Hipp.* 133-4, 201-2, 244-6, 250, 1458; E. *Andr.* 830-2; E. *Hec.* 432, 487, 968-73 (implied); E. *El.* 1227, 1231; E. *Supp.* 110, 286-7; E. *HF* 1111, 1159, 1198, 1202-4, 1226, 1231; E. *Ion* 967; E. *IT* 1207, 1218; E. *Phoe.* 1490-1; E. *Or.* 42-3, 166, 280, 294, 467-8, 957-9; E. *IA* 1118, 1122-3.

wedding clothing, see death clothing

white clothing: A. *Supp.* 719-20; E. *Alc.* 923; E. *Phoe.* 322-6; E. *Hel.* 1186-7

wolfskin: [E.] *Rh.* 201-11

wreath, see **garland**

young-looking clothing: E. *Alc.* 1050

Bibliography

Abbreviations

TGrF = B. Snell, R. Kannicht, S.L. Radt (eds), *Tragicorum Graecorum Fragmenta.* Göttingen (1971-2004).
LIMC = *Lexicon Iconographicum Mythologiae Classicae.* Zurich and Munich (1981-1999).
LSJ = H.G. Liddell and R. Scott, *A Greek-English Lexicon*, 9th edn, revised and augmented by H.S. Jones, with a revised supplement ed. P.G.W. Glare. Oxford (1996).

Works cited

Alföldi, A. (1955), 'Gewaltherrscher und Theaterkönig', in K. Weitzmann (ed.), *Late Classical and Medieval Studies in honour of Albert Matthias Friend, Jr.*, 15-55. Princeton.
Barber, E.J.W. (1991), *Prehistoric Textiles*. Princeton.
Barber, E.J.W. (1992), 'The peplos of Athena', in J. Neils (ed.), *Goddess and Polis: The Panathenaic Festival in Ancient Athens*, 103-19. Princeton.
Battezzatto, L. (2000), 'Dorian dress in Greek tragedy', *Illinois Classical Studies* 25, 343-62.
Beare, W. (1950), *The Roman Stage*. London.
Beazley, J.D. (1955), 'Hydria fragments in Corinth', *Hesperia* 24, 305-19.
Bieber, M. (1961), *The History of the Greek and Roman Theater*. Princeton.
Brooke, I. (1962), *Costume in Greek Classical Drama*. London.
Cairns, D. (1996), 'Veiling, aidôs, and a red-figure amphora by Phintias', *Journal of Hellenic Studies*, 116, 152-7 with Plate 1.
Carlson, M. (1994a), 'The haunted stage: recycling and reception in the theatre', *Theatre Survey* 35, 5-18.
Carlson, M. (1994b), 'Invisible presences – performance intertextuality', *Theatre Research International* 19, 111-17.
Chaston, C. (2010), *Tragic Props and Cognitive Function*. Leiden and Boston.
Cleland, L. (2005) *The Brauron Clothing Catalogues: texts, analysis, glossary and translation*. Oxford.
Cleland, L., M. Harlow and L. Llewellyn-Jones (2005) (eds), *The Clothed Body in the Ancient World*. Oxford.

143

Cleland, L., G. Davies and L. Llewellyn-Jones (2007), *Greek and Roman Dress from A-Z*. London.

Coarelli, F. (2002) (ed.; tr. P. Cockram), *Pompeii*. New York.

Collard, C., M.J. Cropp and J. Gibert (2004), *Euripides: Selected Fragmentary Plays*, vol. 2. Warminster.

Collard, C., M.J. Cropp and K.H. Lee (1997), *Euripides: Selected Fragmentary Plays*, vol. 1. Warminster.

Croom, A.T. (2000), *Roman Clothing and Fashion*. Stroud.

Csapo, E. (2010), *Actors and Icons of the Ancient Theater*. Chichester, UK.

Csapo, E. and M.C. Miller (2007), *The Origins of Theater in Ancient Greece and Beyond*. Cambridge.

Csapo, E. and W.J. Slater (1994), *The Context of Ancient Drama*. Ann Arbor.

Dingel, J. (1967), *Das Requisit in der griechischen Tragödie* (Diss., Tübingen).

Duncan, A. (2006), *Performance and Identity in the Classical World*. New York.

Edmondson, J.C. and A. Keith (eds) (2008), *Roman Dress and the Fabrics of Roman Culture*. Toronto.

Everson, T. (2004), *Warfare in Ancient Greece: arms and armour from the heroes of Homer to Alexander the Great*. Stroud.

Foley, H. (1980), 'The masque of Dionysos', *Transactions of the American Philological Association* 110, 107-33.

Foley, H. (2000), 'The comic body in Greek art and drama', in B. Cohen (ed.), *Not the Classical Ideal*, 275-311. Leiden.

Forbes, R.J. (1964), *Studies in Ancient Technology* (2nd edn, vol. 4), Leiden.

Garland, R. (1985), *The Greek Way of Death*. London.

Goetsch, S. (1995), 'And what about costume?', *Didaskalia* 2.2 http://www.didaskalia.net/issues/vol2no2/goetsch.html, accessed 30 September 2010

Green, J.R. (1982), 'Dedications of masks', *Revue Archéologique* 2, 237-48.

Green, J.R. (1985), 'A representation of the *Birds* of Aristophanes', in J. Frel and S.K. Morgan (eds), *Greek Vases in the J. Paul Getty Museum* 2, 95-118. Malibu.

Green, J.R. (1991), 'Depicting the theatre in Classical Athens', *GRBS* 32 (1991), 15-50.

Green, J.R. (2002), 'Towards a reconstruction of performance style', in P.E. Easterling and E. Hall (eds), *Greek and Roman Actors: aspects of an ancient profession*, 93-126. Cambridge

Griffith, R.D. (1988), 'Disrobing in the *Oresteia*', *Classical Quarterly* 38, 552-4.

Hall, E. and F. Macintosh (2005), *Greek Tragedy and the British Theatre 1660-1914*. Oxford.

Bibliography

Halliwell, S. (1993), 'The function and aesthetics of the Greek tragic mask', *Drama* 2, 195-211.

Jenkins, I. (1983), 'Dressed to kill', *Omnibus* 5, 29-32.

Kokolakis, M. (1961), *Lucian and Tragic Performances in his Time*. Athens.

Lada-Richards, I. (1999), *Initiating Dionysus*. Oxford.

Lambert, C.M. (2008), *Performing Greek Tragedy in Mask: re-inventing a lost tradition* (PhD thesis, University of London).

Ley, G. (1991), *A Short Introduction to the Ancient Greek Theater*. Chicago.

Linders, T. (1972), *Studies in the Treasure Records of Artemis Brauronia*. Stockholm.

Lissarrague, F. (2010), 'From pot to flat page', in O. Taplin and R. Wyles (eds), *The Pronomos Vase and its Context*, 33-46. Oxford.

Llewellyn-Jones, L. (2001), 'The use of set and costume design in modern productions of ancient Greek drama', Open University essay available at: www2.open.ac.uk/ClassicalStudies/GreekPlays/essays/LLJ1.doc, accessed 10 September 2010.

Llewellyn-Jones, L. (2002) (ed.), *Women's Dress in the Ancient Greek World*. London.

Macleod, C. (1974), 'Euripides' rags', *Zeitschrift fur Papyrologie und Epigraphik* 15, 221-2.

Marshall, C.W. (2001a), 'The costume of Hecuba's attendants', *Acta Classica* 44, 127-36.

Marshall, C.W. (2001b), 'The next time Agamemnon died', *Classical World* 95, 59-63.

Miller, M.C. (1997), *Athens and Persia in the Fifth Century BC: a study in cultural receptivity*. Cambridge.

Muecke, F. (1982a), '"I know you – by your rags": costume and disguise in fifth-century drama', *Antichthon* 16, 17-34.

Muecke, F. (1982b), 'A portrait of the artist as a young woman', *Classical Quarterly* 32, 41-55.

Osborne, R. (1997), 'Men without clothes: heroic nakedness and Greek art', *Gender & History* 9, 504-28.

Pickard-Cambridge, A.W. (1968) (revised edn with supplement by J. Gould and D.M. Lewis), *The Dramatic Festivals of Athens*. Oxford.

Podlecki, A.J. (1989), *Aeschlyus: Eumenides*. Warminster.

Quinn, M. (1990), 'Celebrity and the semiotics of acting', *New Theatre Quarterly* 22, 154-61.

Rehm, R. (1994), *Marriage to Death: the conflation of wedding and funeral rituals in Greek tragedy*. Princeton.

Reinhold, M. (1970), *History of Purple as a Status Symbol in Antiquity*. Brussels.

Revermann, M. (2006), *Comic Business*. Oxford.

Robson, J. (2004), 'Aristophanes on how to write tragedy: what you wear is what you are', in F. McHardy, J. Robson and D. Harvey (eds), *Lost Dramas of Classical Athens: Greek tragic fragments*, 173-88. Exeter.

Robson, J. (2005), 'New clothes, a new you: clothing and character in Aristophanes', in L. Cleland, M. Harlow and L. Llewellyn-Jones (eds), 65-74. Oxford.

Roccos, L.J. (2006), *Ancient Greek Costume: an annotated bibliography, 1784-2005*. North Carolina and London.

Scullion, S. (2002), ' "Nothing to do with Dionysus": tragedy misconceived as ritual', *Classical Quarterly* 52, 102-37.

Sebasta, J.L. and L. Bonfante (1994) (eds), *The World of Roman Costume*. Wisconsin.

Sofer, A. (2003), *The Stage Life of Props*. Ann Arbor.

Sourvinou-Inwood, C. (1997) 'Medea at a shifting distance: images and Euripidean tragedy', in J. Clauss and S.I. Johnston (eds), *Medea: essays on Medea in myth, literature, philosophy and art*, 253-96. Princeton.

Stone, L. (1980), *Costume in Aristophanic Comedy*. New York.

Taplin, O. (1977), *The Stagecraft of Aeschylus*. Oxford.

Taplin, O. (1978), *Greek Tragedy in Action*. London.

Taplin, O. (1993), *Comic Angels and Other Approaches to Greek Drama through Vase Painting*. Oxford.

Taplin, O. (2007) *Pots and Plays: interactions between tragedy and Greek vase-painting of the fourth century BC*. Los Angeles.

Taplin, O and R. Wyles (eds), *The Pronomos Vase and its Context*. Oxford.

Thalmann, W.G. (1980), 'Xerxes' rags: some problems in Aeschylus' *Persians*', *American Journal of Philology* 101, 260-82.

Vervain, C. and D. Wiles (2001), 'The masks of Greek tragedy as point of departure for modern performance', *New Theatre Quarterly* 67, 254-72.

Vickers, M.J. (1999), *Images on Textiles: the weave of fifth-century Athenian art and society*. Konstanz.

Wiles, D. (1991), *The Masks of Menander: sign and meaning in Greek and Roman performance*. Cambridge.

Wiles, D. (2007), *Mask and Performance in Greek Tragedy*. Cambridge.

Wilson, P. (2000), *The Athenian Institution of the Khoregia: the chorus, the city, and the stage*. Cambridge.

Winnington-Ingram, R. (1969), 'Euripides, *poietes sophos*', *Arethusa* 2, 127-42.

Wyles, R. (2007) *The Stage Life of Costume in Euripides'* Telephus, Heracles, *and* Andromeda (PhD thesis, University of London).

Wyles, R. (2008) 'The symbolism of costume in ancient pantomime', in E. Hall and R. Wyles (eds), *New Directions in Ancient Pantomime*, 61-86. Oxford.

Wyles, R. (2010a), 'Towards theorising the place of costume in performance reception', in E. Hall and S. Harrop (eds), *Theorising Performance*, 171-80. London.

Wyles, R. (2010b), 'The tragic costumes', in O. Taplin and R. Wyles (eds), *The Pronomos Vase and its Context*, 231-53. Oxford.

Translations used

Babbitt, F.C. (1936), *Plutarch: Moralia*, vol. IV. Loeb. Cambridge, MA.

Barlow, S. (1986), *Euripides: Trojan Women*. Warminster.

Barlow, S. (1996), *Euripides: Heracles*. Warminster.

Collard, C. (1991), *Euripides: Hecuba*. Warminster.

Coleridge, E.P. (1938) in W.J. Oates and E. O'Neill (eds), *Euripides: The Complete Greek Drama*, vol. 1. New York.

Conybeare, F.C. (1912), *Philostratus: The Life of Apollonius of Tyana*. London.

Csapo, E. and W.J. Slater (1994), *The Context of Ancient Drama*. Ann Arbor.

Davie, J. (2003), *Euripides: Medea and Other Plays*. London.

De Sélincourt, A. (1996), *Herodotus: Histories*. London.

Fowler, H.W. and F.G. Fowler (1905), *The Works of Lucian of Samosata*, vol. 2. Oxford.

Harman, A.M. (1936), *Lucian*, vol. 5. Cambridge, MA.

Lattimore, R. (1961), *Homer: Iliad*. Chicago.

Lloyd-Jones, H. (1982), *Aeschylus: Oresteia*. London.

Lloyd-Jones, H. (1996), *Sophocles: Fragments*. Loeb. Cambridge, MA.

Möllendorff, P. von (2001), 'Frigid enthusiasts: Lucian on writing history', *Proceedings of the Cambridge Philological Society* 47, 116-40.

Penella, R.J. (2000), *The Private Orations of Themistius*. Berkeley, CA.

Rudd, N. (1997), *Horace: Satires and Epistles*. Penguin.

Seaford, R. (2001), *Euripides: Bacchae*. Warminster.

Sommerstein, A. (1973), *Aristophanes: Lysistrata/The Acharnians/The Clouds*. London.

Sommerstein, A. (1996), *Aristophanes: Frogs*. Warminster.

Sommerstein, A. (2001), *Aristophanes: Thesmophoriazusae*. Warminster.

Sommerstein, A. (2009), *Aeschylus: The Persians and other plays*. London.

Warner, R. (1972), *Thucydides: History of the Peloponnesian War*. London.

West, M.L (1987), *Euripides: Orestes*. Warminster.

Wright, W.C. (1989), *Philostratus: Lives of the Sophists*. Cambridge, MA.

Index